INVEST YOUR HEARTBEATS WISELY

INVEST YOUR HEARTBEATS WISELY

Practical, Philosophical, and Principled Leadership Concepts for Business and Life

THEO ETZEL

GREENLEAF
BOOK GROUP PRESS

Published by Greenleaf Book Group Press
Austin, Texas
www.gbgpress.com

Distributed by Greenleaf Book Group

For ordering information or special discounts for bulk purchases, please contact Greenleaf Book Group at PO Box 91869, Austin, TX 78709, 512.891.6100.

Design and composition by Greenleaf Book Group and Kim Lance
Cover design by Greenleaf Book Group and Kim Lance
Cover images: top heart: nurulanga/iStock collection/Thinkstock;
jar hearts: ©iStockphoto.com/Roberto Rizzo;
jar: kostsov/iStock Collection/Thinkstock

Cataloging-in-Publication data is available.

Print ISBN: 978-1-62634-254-5

eBook ISBN: 978-1-62634-255-2

Part of the Tree Neutral® program, which offsets the number of trees consumed in the production and printing of this book by taking proactive steps, such as planting trees in direct proportion to the number of trees used: www.treeneutral.com

TreeNeutral

Printed in the United States of America on acid-free paper

16 17 18 19 20 21   10 9 8 7 6 5 4 3 2 1

First Edition

*This is dedicated to my father, Ted Etzel Jr.,
who taught me the value of lifelong learning; dedication;
commitment to principles; love of God, family, and country;
and sacrifice when life demanded it. He was a true role model
and mentor to me in business, being a husband, and being a
father. He never hesitated to invest his heartbeats in me,
and, for that, I am forever grateful.*

*"In all thy ways acknowledge Him
and He shall direct thy path."*

PROVERBS 3:6

*"As you go through life,
no matter your goal,
keep your eye upon the doughnut
and not upon the hole."*

JAMES FRANKLIN MILLER III,
MENTOR AND CLOSE FAMILY FRIEND,
WHO WAS FOND OF REPEATING
THE "OPTIMIST'S CREED"

CONTENTS

PREFACE

The word *invest* means something different to each of us. It could trigger thoughts of financial options. It could represent emotional commitment in a relationship or mission. But either way, if we invest in something, we usually expect something in return—if not for us, for our business, our organization, our cause, or the greater good. To invest, you must be willing to devote time and money, your heartbeats, to what you wish to advance. And because heartbeats are finite, investing them wisely is significantly important.

So why do some executives thrive while others fail, even though they might follow similar business plans and have distinct market advantages? How can infusing your company with faith, ethical behavior, accountability, and transparent personal values be transformative to its success? It all begins with wise investments.

Making a successful investment requires more than dollars and cents. In *Invest Your Heartbeats Wisely*, I've outlined the experiences and methods that have helped me and my teammates grow our company steadily and keep it growing, despite some of the most challenging economic times on record. Although the purpose of any business is profit, in this book I'll show you how maintaining integrity in your business isn't only possible; it is imperative to the success of your ventures.

In one of America's business success stories, my team and I took our company from a $2.7 million local operation to a $45 million regional heating, ventilation, air conditioning, and refrigeration powerhouse. But, personally, I spent years—many times unknowingly—preparing for that role, working as a corporate real estate developer, hospitality organization vice president, and then a business owner. Whether you're a small business entrepreneur, a veteran executive, a CEO, or a business student just beginning to blaze your trail through life, I hope the lessons I've learned along the way will help you on your own path to greater success, purpose, and fulfillment.

—THEO ETZEL

ACKNOWLEDGMENTS

As would be true with most authors, there are far too many people to thank for my success and mentoring than these pages allow. I have been blessed to be surrounded and influenced by people who showed me strong character and perseverance, in good and bad times, who taught me the honest way was the best way. The dedicated people who work with me, side by side—a true dream team—made it possible for me to excel in business and find the fun in it. Thank you to all the people willing to share their experience with me and allow me to learn from them.

Roots run deep, and the lessons I learned through the examples my parents showed me are the legacy they leave now that they are together in heaven. World War II and the Depression were large, central influences in their lives, and those strong, patriotic, and sacrificial characteristics were not lost in my upbringing. Christian love abounded in my home. Although I was an only child, I was shown how personal responsibility, self-sufficiency through work, and the blessings from sharing with others made a life more fulfilling—traits I still embrace today and try to model to others. Their wisdom courses through my veins.

My wife's family embraced me at the young age of sixteen, when our paths were brought together. My father-in-law and mother-in-law are truly my second set of parents. They have been instrumental in shaping who I am and in my opportunity to have a larger, extended family. I would not be the person I am today without their Godly influence on me. They have always believed in me, supported me, invested their heartbeats in me, and—most important—loved me.

Second only to God, family is the most important motivator for me. My wife, Kim, and our children, Charles and Kristen, have stood by me in the ups and downs of life and are a paramount source of joy in my life. What a support system they have been for me; they have certainly been a key motivator for me to hold myself accountable for my actions. The Lord is working on me through them all the time.

Hope is the greatest gift anyone can give another person. Without hope, the reason for trying to move forward does not exist. I am so thankful that the greatest hope available to the human race has been given through the sacrificial love of God through His son, Jesus Christ. With our hope secured in the life, death, and resurrection of Christ, we can face life with the full faith and belief of eternal life and of the presence of the Holy Spirit in us on this earth. I thank you, God, for the people you placed in my life at the right times to help me on my continuing journey.

CHAPTER 1

THE VALUE
OF HEARTBEATS

"I am not a product of my circumstances.
I am a product of my decisions."

—STEPHEN COVEY

The best leadership advice I ever received wasn't from a Fortune 500 CEO or business expert. It was from my mother.

"Son, spend your heartbeats wisely," said this woman who had served in the civilian services, screening letters during World War II. In her wisdom, my mother knew that each of us has only so many heartbeats on this earth. Behind every hour we work and every dollar we spend is a heartbeat. We trade heartbeats like currency. They give us buying power in the grand scheme of life. That's why, as a leader, the very best thing you can do for yourself and your company is to make sure what you're doing is really worth trading for those heartbeats.

Each of us has only so many heartbeats on this earth.

Think of each heartbeat, of each moment, as a gift. When people give you a gift, they have traded their heartbeats to allow you to receive something from them. It may not be what you would have chosen, but it represents a part of them. So, too, does a gift you give to others; it is a reflection of a personal resource that you traded so that they could have something special from you. Each of us has a different idea of value or worth in spending heartbeats. My advice is to make sure that you believe, in your innermost being, that what you are trading your heartbeats for is worth it.

Why is this so important? The most successful leaders understand the lesson my parents taught me as a young boy—that everything doesn't revolve around me. Keep in mind that when people give you money for your business, they have given you their own heartbeats in exchange. Measure those with respect.

Leadership Heartbeats

- Spend your heartbeats wisely.
- Make sure what you do in your life and in your company is really worth trading for those heartbeats.

CHAPTER 2

TRAITS OF EFFECTIVE LEADERSHIP

*"If your actions inspire others to
dream more, learn more, do more, and
become more, you are a leader."*

—JOHN QUINCY ADAMS

I am a member of Vistage, an international association of CEOs, executives, and business owners of companies that generate $3 million or more in annual revenue and that employ at least five people. Those of us involved with the organization were sad to lose Vistage leader Charles "Red" Scott in 2013, but he left a legacy that continues to help us manage things and lead people. I follow his eight principles of success. He argued that every leader should possess

- a feeling of being lucky;
- a sense of greatness;
- a strong work ethic, a willingness to work long hours, persistence;
- a sense of urgency;
- enthusiasm;
- the willingness to take risks;
- high self-esteem; and
- a belief in God.

Each of these traits gives leaders the ability to address problems as they come up and to do so in a way that is not only best for the company but also best for the people working in it. Leaders with a feeling of being lucky will be more likely to take risks when a situation calls for it, but they will also be more appreciative—and protective—of what they have built in the company. A sense of greatness and high self-esteem gives them the confidence to set lofty goals and achieve them. A strong work ethic ensures that leaders will do the work that is necessary for success, and when that's combined with the enthusiasm to follow through and a sense of urgency, leaders are able to get things done quickly and decisively. Finally, a belief in God gives leaders a set of principles to live by and to lead their companies by so that they can achieve financial success in a moral fashion—through hard work, good decisions, and by treating their employees and customers well.

Manage things. Lead people.

Rear Admiral Grace Hopper (December 1906–January 1992) was a US naval officer. Dr. Hopper was an American computer scientist and one of the first people to develop a compiler for computer programming. She is credited with popularizing machine independent programming,[1] which led to the development of one of the first high-level programming languages, COBOL. She also coined the term *debugging*, which is still used today.

She is famous for many things, but one of my favorite quotes attributed to her goes like this: "You manage things; you lead people."[2]

Things can be moved around, and they stay where you put them. They (usually) do what you tell them to and rarely complain. People have goals of their own, a will, and feelings. In order to do their jobs well, people need to be convinced that what they are doing is important and for some purpose, and it helps to have someone they respect in charge.

In one of my previous corporate positions, my leader was a guy who used his job to avoid his situation at home. He had placed personal ambition in front of family time and spent more hours at work and away from home than was needed. It becomes easier to slight our loved ones because we feel they will easily forgive us, or we simply don't want to face what's happening at home, so we avoid those issues by working more. Neither is a good habit.

I didn't respect that. The sad thing is that a lot of people fall into this easy trap. Respect in the workplace starts with the leader, with you. Here are the top tried-and-true tips that I've come to rely on to earn and maintain the respect of my employees:

- Be yourself.
- Don't call yourself the boss.
- Don't lead with fear.
- Don't take yourself too seriously.
- Motivate; don't dictate.

Be yourself

I once read an article about the president of Costco and how he prefers to be treated like every other worker. His nametag reads only "Bob." I share his views on being approachable. If you can extend this philosophy through your business, then your employees will strive to work with you, not against the grain. Your employees still know you are in charge and hold power, but it is not necessary to announce it everywhere you go in a self-aggrandizing way. That just makes you less approachable and puts a wall around you—invisible to you but very visible to others. Approachability equals information; walls will leave you in the dark.

Don't call yourself the boss

Just the other day, someone said, "Hi boss!" to me, and although I appreciate the respect, I hate the word *boss*. The word has a negative connotation and is inextricably linked with power. I think that word should be struck from employee–employer relationships. The word *boss* has its roots in the Dutch word for "master." The connotation of the boss from a few decades ago is someone who leads out of fear and an abuse of power. Clearly, this does not resonate with people today (although some still try), and the younger workers entering the workforce do not respond to this type of treatment. My personal preference is not to be known as the boss.

Seek the right people, with the right talents
for the position, equip them as needed for the job,
and then get out of their way.

My job is to build stars, not be the star. I'm not the star player; I'm just the coach. If you have or want to have a coach mentality as a leader as I do, you must be prepared to seek the right people, with the right talents for the position, equip them as needed for the job, and then get out of their way so they can perform. This does not mean forgetting about them—quite the opposite. It means being there to support their efforts and making certain they are on the path to success for both the company and themselves.

Don't lead with fear

The management/leadership philosophy that it is better to be feared than loved keeps people off base and in fear of their employer and position. It keeps them subservient, but I reject that as a form of proper leadership. You can be strong as a leader and well respected without relying on fear. To me, leading through fear is just a sign of weakness in your own leadership skills and shows a lack of understanding for underlying leadership principles.

Leading with fear will crush your business. Employees who have to carry around the weight of fear in the workplace will certainly always seek the safest way to perform their duties. This may not always be the best for the business when innovative thought is required, as it is in today's global environment. Innovation and idea exchange are stifled if people are in constant fear of you, for their job security, or of challenging the status quo.

I go around every morning and step into offices and say hi like every other employee. I want my employees to respect me but not to be intimidated by me. We shouldn't be buddies, but we should have a friendly professional relationship, in which we respect each other. This way, they are open to my leadership and willing to do their best work for me and for the company.

Don't take yourself too seriously

It's okay to laugh at work. I have a self-deprecating humor and poke fun at myself, but I can still maintain a serious attitude when it comes to running the business. Balance the two, and you'll have a working environment that's tough to beat. When downturns in business occur and tough decisions on spending must be made, it's usually not a laughing matter. In fact, the people around you would probably think you are taking the situation too lightly and are not really concerned about them or their future if you reacted lightheartedly. In the more normal, day-to-day business activities, being able to share a laugh or not-so-serious moment with people brings the team together. Knowing what situation calls for what reaction and behavior is the responsibility of all leaders in an organization.

Motivate; don't dictate

One of the ways you show respect for your employees is to give them a reason for the task you are asking them to perform. People want to be inspired and not simply told what to do, where to do it, when to do it by, and how. Yes, people want guidelines and a safe zone to operate in; boundaries are key concepts that all of us want for general direction. Inspirational leaders motivate through big ideas and by giving purpose, not by brandishing a stick.

> *People want to be inspired and not simply told what to do, where to do it, when to do it by, and how.*

If you dictate to your employees what they should do and how they should do it, if you micromanage and simply expect them to obey without thought, your employees may do what you tell them, but their hearts won't be in it. They'll only invest the heartbeats necessary to get the job done to its minimum requirements and move on to the next assignment.

However, if you motivate them, give them a purpose within the company, and allow them a personal stake in the work, they will shine. They'll work harder because they have a reason other than being told to work. They'll work more carefully and invest more of their heartbeats to meet their own career goals, which when they are aligned with the company's goals and yours, benefits everyone.

At a kickoff meeting on an air conditioning installation job for a big general contractor, we—all the subcontractors—were assembled in a circle. We knew this was a fast-track job. The general contractor's project manager led off the meeting with a series of threats about penalties for delays and over-time demands, ranting and raving for no reason, and cursing at every turn. We were shown no respect, and it was clear that he did not want to be doing this project at all. No motivation was handed out that day. We shook our heads in amazement after the meeting. Conversely, I've been to kickoff meetings where ideas for cooperation and efficiency were solicited and respected. People felt needed and desired. And they worked harder, faster, and better in that environment.

Employees don't want to be berated. Embrace cooperation and never forget to let your team know you have faith in them to complete the job in a way that will best benefit the client and, in turn, the company.

It's important to maintain a relationship as a leader in which accountability can be demanded of the team without resorting to scare tactics. In the end, the work must be done, and in order to ensure that it is, a leader must understand the difference between being friendly—professional but pleasant—and being buddies—where the relationship overshadows the work—with your staff.

Recently, a high school student asked me whether I was an authoritarian leader or a friend to my staff. My answer was that I am a friendly authoritarian. At the end of the day, I have to be an authority, but I prefer to be approachable and friendly. However, I am not friends as high school students would perceive it with my staff, because that would diminish my objectivity: I might not be able to make the right decisions for the company.

Optimistic leadership

Hope is not a business plan: Saying "I hope things turn around" will not actually make them turn around. However, hope, as part of a positive attitude, must be central to any leader—in good times and bad. Whether we like it or not, we leaders are on stage all the time in front of our staff. We may not even know we are on stage, or we may take it for granted, but our coworkers take their cues from us every day. If we do not show a winning, positive attitude about our business, especially when tough decisions are called for, the resulting negative attitudes in the office and in the field will spell disaster for the organization.

If you are not feeling 100 percent one day, maybe it's one of your less glorious days; if you're not ready to walk into the building and say, "It's showtime!" then stay away from the office that day until you can get yourself back to being the leader you know you need to be. No one can be "on" all the time. We are all human. I've learned that if I walk into the office glum that day—acting like Eeyore—I'm going to have a passel of Eeyores.

As a leader, you have to be consistently positive in your outlook and attitude and must demonstrate that. It's all part of being on stage, part of what you are called to do. If you want others to mirror that, you have to be that person. Don't be a hypocrite; live and lead by your values. There is no easy way to stay true to your principles; you have to work at it. Part of that journey comes from finding the joy in living how God wants you to live, which gives you more ability to say no to the pressures of society and the world.

Be humble

In business and life, we are called to be humble rather than prideful. This ties in with my other tips as well: If you are humble, it's easier to be yourself, and you're not likely to want to be called the boss. Successful leaders know they cannot be self-centered or prideful and at the same time remain open to corrective lessons—much less advice—from their colleagues and especially not from their employees. This advice might be something you would never have thought of on your own, and it might be brilliant.

This is why you, as the leader of your organization, need to be a good listener. You have to be able to listen and see things from other people's viewpoint to understand what's important to them. More important, if you're so full of pride that you can't take constructive criticism, then you can't listen and receive good advice.

In the end, you'll have to make a decision, and people will probably have some variations on their approach to the situation. But all input should be considered in formulating the final decision. I'm not preaching leading by consensus. While that can take place, and it's great when it does, that is not the total goal here. Being open to other viewpoints and giving proper consideration usually yields a better decision.

I've been guilty of starting to run so fast I have simply forgotten to stop and ask the folks on the front lines how they would handle something. After my solution proved not to be stellar, the *duh* moment hit, and I sought their input. Our customers were much better off with their solution, and as a result, we increased our referral rate because we were able to be more responsive.

Listening allowed me to learn from other people and provided a good learning environment. I learned the right thing to do, which sends the right message to people.

There is a difference between having pride in your work and being prideful. I've not seen a lot of people who were full of pride make it for very long. They usually trip themselves up or something trips them up. Life humbles everyone, so it's better to start out that way and use it to your advantage.

Leadership is all about balance. Leaders must maintain a balance between methodical processes that are understood and implementable. They must also recognize the value of hiring individuals who possess some exuberance. Wild exuberance without structure doesn't work in business. By the same token, a strictly methodical leader who is closed off from being adaptable, doesn't have a fun side, or has poor listening skills is going to provide a poor environment in which to work. That leader will have a hard time leading people.

It all comes down to a leader's ability to be relatable to the team. Without these skills, leaders will miss opportunities because they give the impression that other opinions don't matter. And they will have an uphill battle getting the team to be enthused about following them, because there is no real connection between the team and leaders like that.

Leadership Heartbeats

- Manage things. Lead people.
- Give your team members a reason for the task you are asking them to perform.
- Understand the difference between being friendly and being buddies with your team members.
- Live and lead by your values.
- Listen more; talk less.

CHAPTER 3

LEADERSHIP IN PRACTICE

"I am not afraid of an army of
lions led by a sheep; I am afraid of
an army of sheep led by a lion."

—ALEXANDER THE GREAT

Contrary to the old saying, the devil is *not* in the details; the devil appears where the details have been overlooked. Nowhere is that more true than when a leader begins to get sloppy. When you don't sweat the small things, that's when you begin to overlook the big things. Realizing that there are minor erosions in the profit margin and failing to address the situation quickly—or worse, rationalizing it away—can lead to a major cash problem down the road and potentially jeopardizes the life of the company.

Don't misunderstand: This is not a license to microman-age. It is a reminder to focus on the important aspects of your business. As a leader I say, "This is how we will do business." But then I equip my staff with the right tools and let them do their jobs. I don't micromanage. I want to set people up for success—to do business and live in that business world aligned with beliefs and personal philosophies that differenti-ate between right and wrong.

Focus on the important aspects of your business.

Losing focus on the details happens often in the service sector, where customers frequently set low expectations for the level of service they expect. For example, what seems like a little detail to an organization may be a big detail to the consumer.

This may seem to contradict the idea of carefully invest-ing your heartbeats. However, I don't mean that you should obsess over every operational detail. As the leader, you must be accountable for the details that will set you apart. Customers know what they want, but they don't expect people to fulfill that. If you return their phone call, show up on time, deliver what you said you would deliver, customers will think you're the greatest and will respond with loyalty.

Decisive leadership

Some decisions are simply not fun. I'd rather have days filled with fun than some rock-your-boat decisions that need to be made. Most people don't wake up and look for emotionally uncomfortable situations in which to put themselves. But running from this discomfort leads to ignoring the problem—or the opportunity that the problem presents—and results in a failure to address the immediate situation. A larger bucket of consequences awaits all involved as more time goes by with no action. It could be dealing with a confrontational customer or a difficult employee. Failure to act and to act in an appropriate time frame only exacerbates the problem. Action with conviction is needed.

This is why decisive leadership is necessary. You need to be able to make decisions, make them quickly, and move on to the next item on your agenda. Otherwise, you—and the company—will get bogged down in a single issue. You'll waste all those heartbeats that could be spent on something more important.

Most situations we face are surrounded by fuzzy, extraneous information and opinions. Focusing on the true kernel of the problem usually makes it manageable. Ask questions to reveal the true root of the problem. Many times, it is not one giant problem but a series of smaller ones that have been allowed to fester. Decisively dealing with each smaller component makes dealing with the collective issue much easier.

A lot has been made of the "ready, fire, aim" concept—someone who makes decisions too quickly. It is a balancing act. Delaying a decision can be as detrimental as moving too quickly. Have you ever heard anyone say, "I'm not going to make a decision until I have all the information in front of me"? Let me address that statement.

Finding the fine line between expediency and
knowledge is a sign of leadership maturity.

You'll *never* have all the information in front of you. It would be so nice to have all the information before having to make a decision, but few situations present themselves in full light and with all the facts. We are left to make decisions with varying degrees of knowledge. You have to find some level of knowledge that you're comfortable with—say, 75 percent of the information—and move forward. People who continue to wait for just a little more information suffer from *paralysis by analysis*: Nothing gets done until one more piece of the puzzle is known. The trouble is that we never have enough pieces of the puzzle for the full picture. I'm not suggesting that you jump to conclusions with barely enough information in hand. Time will kill the deal and limit the options available to us when we wait too long, but being decisive with too little understanding can be equally disastrous. Finding the fine line between expediency and knowledge is a sign of leadership maturity.

Stagnant behavior is just as bad for your business as making the wrong decisions too quickly. Delayed decisions do not go away; they only get more complex. Gaining the confidence to make timely decisions is a practiced art.

I'd rather pass on a good deal and wake up tomorrow and kick myself one time and say, "Next time, I'll make a better decision," than make a bad deal, only to wake each morning thereafter and kick myself because I still own that bad deal.

Avoiding the dreaded "ostrich complex"

It's a common misconception that ostriches bury their heads in the sand. This is the origin of the "ostrich complex"—the idea that you can hide your head, ignore your problems, and they'll go away. To the detriment of their businesses, some CEOs use this approach when they're faced with difficult decisions. Disasters result when issues are not met head-on, with clear, decisive action. In fact, when a CEO leaves a problem to solve itself, the problem most often grows, and the organization loses time, money, and manpower when they finally solve it—or fail to. Avoid this management strategy like the plague. Given enough time, ignoring a problem can wreck your business.

In addition, leaders who bury their heads are no leaders at all. In these situations, leaving a problem to fix itself compromises the image of the organization internally and externally. I call this the "feel better now" syndrome—a short-lived feeling because the weight of indecision mounts and anxiety builds with every passing day. Avoiding tough decisions leads to inefficient operations and a directionless corporate atmosphere.

You may be reading this and saying, "Well, I'd never bury my head in the sand," but it's more tempting than you think.

Not facing a problem is often a far more comfortable solution than dealing with it with steadfast determination. Leaders who play ignorant to detrimental issues aren't heading to any safe zone: Indeed, they are only postponing an even worse feeling of discomfort and ineffective leadership. And worst of all, as time passes, the choices available to you to correct those issues decrease.

Ignorance, not following through, not stepping up—it's a cycle of discomfort, frustration, and regret that may grip the leader and also plague the organization. This behavior is evidence of a pattern of weak leadership.

When I first started in business, I had a mentor who was in the hotel development field. His number one philosophy was that time kills all deals. In other words, opportunities will fall by the wayside, and problems will grow when people just let time pass. Most often, fear, avoidance of emotional discomfort, or a desire to have all the information before making a decision is what causes leaders to bury their heads in the sand. And I, too, have fallen into that trap.

The most common example of this is when we have an employee that we know, in our heart of hearts, is not a team player and needs to go, or a partner in a firm who is not headed in the same direction as you. I have tried to justify leaving these kinds of people in place and working through the situation. But after time, everyone knows what needs to be done, and they are waiting for you to act. Failing to act sends the wrong message; you are accepting below-average behavior, and you become known by what you tolerate. However, experience is a wonderful teacher. The key is learning from, and not repeating, those experiences.

Face your fear of failure

It takes discipline to stay and face the battle rather than run and hide or ignore it, and it takes practice—with focus, discipline, action, and the ability to overcome your fear of failure—to continually move forward and make the proper decisions. These attributes can help you determine the true nature of a problem and take the necessary steps to remedy it. By dealing with the issues, examining options, and asking advice from trusted sources, you can systematically address the problem. This is where deliberate thought and focus come together to help formulate an action plan.

Fear is a good thing to possess in many instances. It heightens our awareness of our surroundings. It should make us take appropriate action. However, when a leader experiences the fear of making a wrong decision or of failure and then chooses to ignore the situation in hopes of it going away, that form of fear is dangerous for the organization. The fear of not being seen as perfect or being able to make the perfect decision every time is not healthy for leaders or the people around them.

For example, at Conditioned Air, we once set out to introduce a product that would monitor conditions in a home or office while people were away and send alerts if the conditions got out of norm. We delayed the product's introduction into the marketplace while trying to get everything about it perfect—the look, the function, the name, the package, all of which are decidedly important. But we took too long and got scooped by bigger players and boxed out of the opportunity. Our fear of putting out a product that was good but not perfect cost us a place in the market.

People know leaders are not perfect. Most, if not all, have had some form of failure. Your staff and customers will accept that as long as you face the day-to-day challenges head-on and not with your backside to the sky. I'll take an imperfect decision maker over a perfectionist afraid to pull the trigger any day. A Chinese proverb illustrates my point: Fall down six times, get up seven. Mistakes happen, but it is better to proactively fail than to fail by avoiding action altogether.

Focus on the heart of the matter, have the
discipline to stand in there and face the music,
and take action to correct the situation.

Focus, discipline, and action are the three steps you must take in order to pull your head out of the sand, and facing your fear keeps your head up to begin with. Focus on the heart of the matter, have the discipline to stand in there and face the music, and take action to correct the situation. The feeling of relief from conquering an obstacle that seemed daunting is enormous. And the best part is that this is real relief with lasting benefits for the company but also for you.

Transparent leadership: WYSIWYG

I am a fairly private person. I don't readily share all my personal information with people. I'm not trying to be standoffish. Rather, I'm just guarded as to how much to reveal and how fast. I am, though, transparent so that people see consistency with who I am through my actions. The acronym WYSIWYG—*what you see is what you get*—is appropriate for leadership; people want to know you are real, have real triumphs, and have real disappointments. And being genuine with people is the greatest gift we can give one another in our interactions.

One sure way to show your genuine approach to leadership is to lead by example. People see and react to action. When the leader takes decisive action to solve problems, his employees think they should also take action. If the leader is seen as a decisive person and not afraid to wrestle with a tough problem, the rest of the company will try to emulate that behavior.

People find whatever they are really seeking. If you're trying to find the right way to do things, you will find the right way to do things. Conversely, when you look for the bad, you'll find that as well. Proverbs 21:21 serves as a great guide: "He who pursues righteousness and love finds light, prosperity, and honor." (Note: All biblical citations in this book refer to the New International Version.) Employees look to their leaders for examples of how to behave, and they will focus on whatever they observe in those leaders. A leader who is accountable to his values and the good of the company encourages this behavior in his employees. We should ask ourselves whether we are acceptable role models in the employee–employer relationship.

One of my favorite characters from Doctor Dolittle is the pushmi-pullyu, pronounced "push me, pull you." Envision trying to push a string across the table. You can't. You have to pull the string across the table. Standing in the back of a company and pushing is not always the best thing. You need to be out front, leading by example.

Servant leadership

In order to lead, you need a structure to support your decisions. For me, biblical principles provide the main support: I try to lead with integrity, respect, and authenticity, but also by providing service. In a 1970 essay called "The Servant as Leader," Robert K. Greenleaf coined the term *servant leadership*, which means that leaders serve their employees in a way that allows those employees to do their jobs to the best of their abilities. I explain the concept to people inside the office this way: "If the customers knew what the problem was, we would be a parts house." For example, when the field technicians call the office for help, they are calling not for their own needs but on behalf of the external customer. When your in-house support speaks to your technician outside of the office, he or she is speaking to the mouthpiece of that customer. So the support representative's respect and assistance should extend to the technician and, therefore, to the customer.

As my wife, Kim, who always speaks from the heart, reminds me, when everyone in high school wanted to be the star, I was the one mowing the field. She'll tell you that receiving the school service award two years in a row meant more to me than the recognition I could have gotten on the football team. My role as a leader has always been about servant leadership, and for me, those heartbeats were well spent.

Leadership Heartbeats

- Decisively deal with each smaller component to make handling the bigger issues easier.
- Don't wait when you know in your heart of hearts that a team member isn't working out. Let that person go.
- It is better to proactively fail than to fail by avoiding action altogether.
- Lead by example.
- Practice servant leadership.

CHAPTER 4

CREATING A
CORPORATE CULTURE
OF ACCOUNTABILITY

*"As iron sharpens iron, so one
person sharpens another."*

—PROVERBS 27:17

A business plan on a shelf doesn't bring a business to life.
Putting that plan into action requires that people—yourself
included—be held accountable for getting things done. You
must take action and encourage your team to do the same.
Give people responsibility for sections of that plan and charge
them with taking action on those areas so that the business will
become a thriving entity. People who are accountable for the

good of the company are essential. At the top of that list, you, the leader, must be accountable to your team, to your customers, and to yourself.

Were we sitting across from one another in a conference room right now, you might be tempted to ask me, "What does Christianity have to do with business? How could it possibly help me earn more money or secure better staff?" Having a set of core values, of beliefs that you live your life and run your company by, is evident to the people you work with. You will attract employees with strong values, and your customers will see it as well.

As a Christian, I try to live my life and conduct myself according to biblical principles. If you're not a person of faith, you may, at this very point, be tempted to stop reading. But I urge you to continue, because—regardless of our differences— we can still learn a lot from people of different faiths and philosophies. I run my companies based on biblical principles, but that doesn't mean everyone has to be Christian, only that I root my business (and life) philosophy in Christian teachings.

I was taught responsibility at a young age. I was fortunate growing up, but I also learned that money doesn't grow on trees. I was exposed to classic manners and upbringing, and those lessons taught me many of life's values, including how utilizing manners truly shows respect for others. At the same time, I was really grounded in faith and how you should treat the resources you are blessed with. I think that's had a huge impact on my life overall and how I approach running a business.

For instance, I trace core values such as integrity back to Proverbs. The Bible offers guidelines for moral living that can be applied to business as well. These values are integral to me, and I make them the core of my businesses, wholly connected to our corporate culture.

It is very important that people understand why your company exists. Even though my most successful company is in heating, ventilation, air conditioning, and refrigeration (HVACR or HVAC), if you ask me what business it is, I'd say we're in the hospitality business. We're here to make people feel comfortable, which means that customers need to feel comfortable with our people—that we're truthful, that we respect property, and so on. For example, when you go to a hotel for a weekend, they are there to make you feel comfortable. You should be happy with their policies and the way they treat you. You can't bring your AC system to our shop. We have to go to your house, and that means we have to show you our hospitality in your own home.

Romans 12:13 speaks to this principle: "Share with God's people who are in need. Practice hospitality." People call us when they are in need. We have a responsibility to treat them with hospitality in all phases of our interaction with them.

My great-grandmother, who was a teacher, would give you a *C* for doing nothing above and beyond the task at hand. Today, people's expectations are so low that they hand out an A if you do the bare minimum. My company has received so many compliments just for doing what we were hired to do.

The funniest compliment we ever got was when our technicians did such a great job cleaning up their work area that the homeowner said she had to clean up her condo just to match the good job they had done.

Because we created a culture in which doing the job—and doing it well—is the norm, that is what our technicians expect and what they communicate to our customers. Through their personal integrity, which is supported by the company's culture, our techs hold themselves accountable to completing their work beyond what customers usually expect.

As for leadership, I've always been very intentional in letting the other leaders in my business know they are on stage. They are example setters, as am I. How I live my life outside this company is how I live my life inside this company. It's not like Friday at 5:00 p.m. comes around and it's time to change into a different person for the weekend. I have a lot of fun and enjoy my life, but I want to earn the respect of my team, and that means behaving in a respectful manner in my personal life. Nothing erodes respect and corporate culture more than a leader who does not lead by example all the time.

An organization is only as good as the
employees and leaders within it.

I enjoy writing positive notes for my team as a motivational tool. In writing one of these notes, I found this acronym, credited to the school system in Fort Meade, Florida: PRIDE stands for *personal responsibility in daily execution*. All people must be personally accountable for what they do each and every day, because an organization is only as good as the employees and leaders within it. When an organization is led properly, each person within it is crucial to the success of the company. The lack of accountability—for both employees and the leadership—is a weak link; it will cause the chain to break.

Making mistakes

When you make a mistake, admit it and move on. Own it. Do something different. If you can't admit a mistake, you will wallow in those mistakes—that's your pride keeping you from success.

What's wrong with saying, "This decision didn't work out, so we're revamping"? People respect this kind of honesty. They'll see that you're smart enough to recognize when something isn't working and confident enough to try a new path. They do not respect people who, to the end, say they were right even when they were wrong.

A few years ago, I had an idea for an ad campaign that involved targeting an audience we typically didn't focus on. It required new ads—about $40,000 in added budget expense—and needed a number of departments to participate in the execution of the plan. My team was spot-on and did as I asked, followed my lead. But the plan was a complete failure and didn't generate any revenue to speak of after the four- or five-month campaign. I had to declare the project a failure in concept, and because I had the idea, was responsible for the overall marketing plan, and controlled the expenses associated with it, I had to own it. I could have blamed it on the staff, but that would have been a lie. I'm responsible. I'm accountable. The team immediately rallied, and we moved on to a new strategy.

This trait is applicable in business as well as with family. People make mistakes. Leaders make mistakes. All people want to hear when someone makes a mistake is "I'm sorry; I messed up. It's my fault, but here's an idea to fix it." Most people will forgive and move on. Humility goes a long way in the eyes of both employees and family. Humility and humbleness do not equate to being a doormat; in fact, they are a sign of strength and confidence. Never being able to admit you were wrong builds an impenetrable wall around you, and people lose respect quickly. Honesty is the best policy.

Communicating corporate culture

There is a culture within every company. It is up to you, as the leader, to make that culture intentional and to decide what culture you want it to be and how you communicate it to the whole organization. You can do this through repetition: It's all about speaking and repeating. Leaders should also show their hospitality within the company. After all, this is where your internal customers—your employees—live. The culture begins and ends with you.

One of the most important things a leader can instill in people is the knowledge of how important the *execution* of a plan is, rather than just the plan itself. You can read this book and think, *Wow! There are a lot of good ideas here,* but if you never take the steps to put something into action, it won't help you make changes in your business or implement practices for success. In a business, whatever the goal or mission is, you have to map out a plan and get people excited about embarking on that plan.

Why is a corporate culture based on values important? People in an organization need structure, or else they will try to implement it themselves. Your staff needs to have boundaries to work within. Companies can be nimble—reactive to the marketplace and able to make adjustments where needed—but that does not mean all team members run in their own direction. There must be an overriding plan through which the leadership points all its staff members toward the same goals. This should be the case regardless of how many departments you have in your company. Define those goals and take aim for cohesiveness. This doesn't mean there can't be teams or people who are creative or outgoing, doing new and innovative things, but, like you, they must serve the good of the company. Everyone must be accountable.

Are you and your team members working for the good of the company? Here are a few questions that might help you determine your answer:

- Being accountable comes from setting expectations on the front end. Are you making sure your staff understands their roles?
- Are you measuring progress along the way?
- Is your team hitting the targets they are supposed to hit?
- Are you holding reeducation meetings to make sure everyone understands timelines, consequences, and how to minimize negative outcomes?

Review this checklist with your team and ask yourselves, *Am I holding myself accountable?*

Leadership Heartbeats

- Be accountable to your team, to your customers, and to yourself.
- Hold your team members accountable, and make sure they hold themselves accountable too.
- Practice PRIDE: Personal responsibility in daily execution.
- Own your mistakes, apologize, and move forward.
- Build a plan, and then execute it.
- Define your company goals and aim for cohesiveness among all team members to reach those goals.

CHAPTER 5

MENTOR MAGIC

*"Mentors are not there to make us
'happy.' They are there to guide us to
the best of their knowledge."*

—SAMIRA DEANDRADE

Part of creating your legacy—and good leadership in general—is mentoring. I've seen firsthand the rewards of becoming a mentor, speaking to and coaching up-and-coming CEOs.

When I first began working, I observed my direct supervisor and noted what I liked and what I didn't like about his management style. So when I began mentoring the man who became the president of Conditioned Air, I knew he would also assess my leadership style.

I've touched on the type of people I like to hire—those who share my values of integrity, respect, and authenticity—and when I met the man who would rise to become our company president, I knew he exemplified those values. There were several markers to indicate that. He served eight years in the US Army. That experience taught him to be independent. He graduated from high school early—so young that his mother had to sign him up for the service in February 1992, when he was seventeen. He was a reservist, spending about a year on active duty—one weekend a month, two weeks a year—and with the GI Bill and money he earned, he persevered through almost eight years to graduate college and become a CPA, all while working full time.

This impressed me—and I recognized the leadership ability in a man who had such patience and tenacity. He will tell you that those early experiences made him who he is today, establishing many of his character traits that led me to bring him aboard.

I came across his resume through an executive recruiter, and he was the last person to interview. By the end of that first day, I offered him the position. He consulted his wife and began the job at Conditioned Air one month later. This was during the start of the great recession in 2006—the year that the local economy in Southwest Florida started its meltdown—and we faced it together as a senior management group. It was a difficult time, but an ideal time to demonstrate leadership and mentoring. Today, he has moved on to owning his own company, and I feel confident that he will be successful and be true to the values he helped instill in our company.

When you help people develop their own
leadership skills, you give them the confidence and
the abilities necessary to continue without you.

Ultimately, your goal should be to lead your team in such a way that you can step away and the company will continue to thrive. Mentoring is one way to do that. When you help people develop their own leadership skills, you give them the confidence and the abilities necessary to continue without you.

Members of my senior management have told me their favorite saying of mine is "When the cart is in the ditch, everyone becomes the ox." As a mentor, I've learned that what I do rubs off on my staff and affects their growth, confidence, management ability, and the wherewithal to run a growing organization.

This applies not only to formal mentoring relationships but also to how you present yourself every day. You have to be careful about how you carry yourself. I would never want someone to say, "I mentored under Theo and have learned a whole host of things I don't want to do." This means practicing and demonstrating your behavior and being consistent.

Being recognized as a good leader, a great husband, a great father is a reflection of what Jesus taught, as related in Paul's letters, as the best possible example of that on earth:

"Husbands, love your wives and do not be harsh with them."

COLOSSIANS 3:19

"Fathers, do not embitter your children,
or they will become discouraged."

COLOSSIANS 3:21

In modeling my own behaviors, all those things are important to me. Leadership is very personal to me in that sense. And it should be to you. Your actions become the legacy your family, friends, and colleagues will remember. People who lead a company should strive to leave it in better shape than when they took over. In that way, your influence will live on and continue to improve the lives affected by your actions.

Another important trait that mentees appreciate is not being micromanaged. People know they must be held accountable to our core values, and that attitude is contagious. Every decision made has to fall in line with the mission statement and our five core values:

Mission Statement

"The Mission of Conditioned Air is to provide products and services in an honorable way that exceeds the expectations of each and every one of our clients within an industry whose reputation is tarnished with mistrust and deceit. Honesty, integrity, respect, and 100% purposeful effort will be afforded all our stakeholders: our CUSTOMERS, our EMPLOYEES, our VENDORS, and our OWNERS."

Five Core Values
- Integrity
- Respect
- Safety
- Purposeful effort
- Exceeding expectations

When all team members are on board with this and willing to take responsibility for their part, there is no need to oversee every aspect of their work.

I have had many mentors in my life. The most important ones, with the longest lasting impressions, weren't afraid to tell me the truth. They did this in a spirit of love as the Bible says to do, but they didn't mince words. At times, those words were hard to hear, their advice difficult to follow. The unvarnished truth makes you look deep inside, and it stings the ego (edging God out). People who hear the words and respond can change for the better. The Bible says many things about how to gain wisdom and improve yourself. Proverbs is great for lessons on wisdom and our need for it:

"Whoever scorns instruction will pay for it, but whoever respects a command is rewarded."

PROVERBS 13:13

One of the most limiting things we can do as leaders is to just jump in and fix a situation rather than fixing the person. There is a huge temptation to solve the problem yourself. Jesus performed miracles, and we know he had the power to perform many more if he had wanted to do so, but more often, he instructed people in how they should live or behave or challenged their laws and belief systems so they could make life-changing improvements inside themselves. I have been guilty of just fixing things and moving on. The problem comes when the situation repeats itself and—guess what—I have to fix it again because I didn't allow people to fix it themselves and learn a new skill.

All organizations have challenges. Life has challenges. When we simply remove a challenge from somebody (I'm not talking about the absence of charity in those situations), we remove the ability for that person to improve. We also lessen the importance of personal responsibility, which can lead to people developing a quick dependency on others to solve their problems. Life's challenges can become the iron we need to help sharpen us. The people you lead must be allowed that opportunity too. Society is full of capable yet dependent people. It is our responsibility to change that through mentoring in our employee mission field.

We're not perfect, but we can learn.

Leaders are called to be mentors for others, whether in family (the most important function you will ever have) or in organizations. Therefore, it is important to learn how to build up a person and at the same time correct, in the spirit of love, behaviors that are destructive. These are self-adaptive traits that develop over time and with trial and error; remember, we're not perfect, but we can learn.

Leadership Heartbeats

- Allow people to fix problems themselves to learn a new skill.
- When the cart is in the ditch, everyone becomes the ox.
- Your actions become the legacy your family, friends, and colleagues will remember.
- When mentoring others, tell the unvarnished truth in the spirit of love.

CHAPTER 6

GETTING A
BUSINESS STARTED

*"Though no one can go back and
make a brand new start, anyone can start from
now and make a brand new ending."*

—CARL BARD

I'm a big believer in the capitalist system. My first business
was a lemonade stand on a bike path in South Miami when I
was ten years old. My parents were encouraging and fronted
the money for the first batch of ingredients, but then I paid
for my supplies with the profits that my sales generated. This
experience taught me the cost of goods and the importance of
a good business location.

Between the ages of fourteen and fifteen, I worked at Bert's Grocery to buy myself my first car. Bert's was a small high-end market in Coconut Grove. Part of my job was to go in the safe to get the caviar for the little old ladies, and my parents had just taken a wine class, so I was able to direct these people to great wines to go with their caviar. I was able to provide solution-based customer service, and it was successful.

When I refer to a solution-based approach, I mean thinking a little bigger than just the immediate need. If I had just gotten them the one item they wanted, then I would have been done. But the fact that I could suggest a wine or cheese to complement the event they were having helped them be successful. I benefited from that as well, because it generated repeat customers who looked for me to help them again.

Through that job, I saved enough money to buy my first car; it was a ten-year-old Buick LeSabre that needed a paint job. Once, I picked up a girl in the car for a date and when I called her after the date, she said, "Do you think you could drive your mom's car next time?" I was proud of that car and the investment of heartbeats it represented. There was no next time.

My wife, Kim, would tell you that I walked my own path in high school. I was never in a club or a clique. I had a wide variety of friends and worked on many projects around school with them. I just invited anyone who shared my vision and morals to walk with me. I drove that clunker of a car to school every day and parked it right up front with pride. I knew there were girls at school that I would never date because of that car.

I knew I had to be true to myself, and when it was time to run a business, I knew I had to do the same.

The barriers to entry are lower today, in many cases, than they used to be, despite the plethora of regulations that can clog the free enterprise system. It is so easy now to incorporate yourself and get into a business. The opportunities are there; you just have to be true to yourself and your values as you plan your business.

Proper alignment between your values and your company is important in steering your company. A vehicle that's not aligned will careen off course, like my beloved car sometimes did. The same can be said of strategy. Alice asked the Cheshire Cat:

> "Would you tell me, please, which way I ought to go from here?"
>
> "That depends a good deal on where you want to get to," said the Cat.
>
> "I don't much care where—" said Alice.
>
> "Then it doesn't matter which way you go," said the Cat.[3]

Focus on the process, not the plan

Business leaders trying to plot the future of their companies without a plan often find their business not going exactly where they intended. Outlining a vision of where you want to go is critical to the success of the organization. But a strategic plan for the organization is key if, and only if, it is a living, breathing document to be used frequently. We really need to start calling this *strategic planning* to indicate the ongoing nature of the refinement and work in progress that this becomes.

A few years ago, I made a business plan. I put a lot of effort into it, but it was a static document, designed to be a set course for the company. It was pretty, had colorful charts, nice graphs, lots of writing and predictions. For the life of me, I don't know what I did with it. Frankly, I never looked at it again. It's gathering dust somewhere, like dinosaur bones in a museum. I felt great when it was done. But it didn't do anything to help my organization—or me—get further down the road. Since that time, I have learned the crucial difference between a *static strategic plan* and *dynamic strategic planning*: If it's static, it's a snapshot; if it's dynamic, it's an ongoing process.

When you prepare a plan and then find that circumstances dictate revamping that plan, you might become anxious. It is natural to feel torn between sticking to the original plan no matter what and making adjustments as market conditions change. However, over the years, I have come to understand that adjustments must be made to various parts of a plan because the world around us changes constantly. Parts of the plan will stand the test of time, and parts need to be reevaluated and reengineered to respond to those changes. If you make a plan and put it on the shelf, you end up with a fairly expensive (it's your time, energy, and missed opportunities) dust collector, as I did.

If it's static, it's a snapshot; if it's
dynamic, it's an ongoing process.

So what exactly is a strategic plan? Although no two plans will ever be assembled or viewed in the same way, there is a basic nature. The strategic plan is an overview of the business and a projection of its future. In business parlance, it's the high-altitude view of the business, the big picture. It includes the past, the present, and the future of the company. Not surprisingly, the past and present are easier to define than the future.

Just how far into the future you want to project comes down to personal choice and judgment. I might not feel comfortable looking twenty-five years ahead, but five to ten years out may be more practical. Again, because this is to be a process and not a snapshot document, certain aspects of the plan will change as time goes by.

Strategic plans reference time frames, money, resources, personnel, location, and the other core features of a business. For example, you may want your company to expand the retrofit/ replacement market over the next two years. This would be stated in terms of expected dollar increases in years one and two, projections of personnel needed to handle the increase in volume, and benchmarks to see whether the plan is on the expected track.

Note that this type of plan does not go into the specifics of how this is to happen. The key people responsible for the work should develop the plan's execution. An owner of a football team may want to go from cellar to stellar in a couple of years, and the head coach will pick the strategy for any one game, but it is typically the special coaching staff that is tasked with developing the play-by-play execution—this is your *tactical plan.*

Neither the strategic plan nor the tactical plan can be developed in a vacuum. They must go hand in hand and require constant communication and feedback to be effective. This is truly some of the most difficult time to justify to ourselves if we do not understand the importance of future planning.

The speed of change around you determines how often you review the overall strategy you have laid out. You might agree that we have seen rapid market changes in the past six months. Therefore, the review process to check whether you are still headed down the right course and whether your goals still fit the market conditions needs to occur more frequently than it would in fairly stable times.

In this case, the size of your company is not the determining factor for success. Rather, it is the company's ability to adjust your plans—both strategic and tactical—to adapt rapidly to the market conditions around you. I'm not advocating abandoning all plans at every change you encounter, but corrections in a timely manner may make the difference between survival and extinction in the quickly changing environment in which we live.

In their book *It's Not the BIG That Eat the SMALL . . . It's the FAST That Eat the SLOW: How to Use Speed as a Competitive*

Tool in Business (HarperCollins, 2002), Jason Jennings and Laurence Haughton make the great observation that the traditional thinking that big companies always dominate small companies is quickly going by the wayside. Their contention is that fast, nimble companies can outperform the slow-to-react ones. Seeing trends ahead of others and having the willingness to act on those trends will lead to winning the race. They believe, as I do, that change for the sake of change, or speed without direction, is reckless and hasty. The direction comes from having a strategy in place and goals set.

Seeing trends ahead of others and having the willingness
to act on those trends will lead to winning the race.

For the planning process to be effective, communication is essential. This is not a hand of cards in poker that you play close to your vest. Sharing the strategic plan with your team is critical to having everybody understand where you want the business to go. This facet of the process can be one of the hardest to master, because the message needs to be repeated regularly for new people who come on board. They won't know your vision for the future of your company. Even veterans of your organization need to be reminded of where you want to go. In times of rapid change, people want to know the plan to get a sense of security. I've struggled with this myself, but it's worth the effort.

The old adage "what gets measured, gets done" is also true

in the strategic planning process. A plan with benchmarks and a review of where you are relative to your benchmarks leads to better decision making. More than likely, this involves comparing the budget with actual numbers or evaluating on the basis of key performance indicators.

During the review process, you may need to adjust these numbers along with the strategic plan. Also, this is a very timely way to measure the tactical plan and its effectiveness in heading toward the strategic goals. The road from where you are today to where you want to be is not always straight. In fact, I believe that the straight road would lead right over a cliff and into the abyss. It's the curving road that navigates around the mountain's edge. Adjustments in the plan are necessary along the journey.

I've been discussing strategic planning for business, but that same high-altitude view can be used for your personal life as well. Step back and look at where you want to go, what you want to be doing, and by what age you see these things coming to fruition. Certainly, as business owners and leaders, these personal goals can have a direct impact on the strategic planning of the business. The reflective nature of this at the personal level can have a life-changing impact on people.

Like almost anything, starting a planning process is the hardest part. Keep in mind that most people are hungry for direction. The key is sitting down away from the office and talking about the future and what that can look like. Write some of these things down and then ask the question "What do we have to do today to position our company to look like that in the future?"

It's a working-it-backward process in the beginning and then a check-and-balance process along the way. The adjustments become easier to understand as the benchmarks are met or missed. Be aware that the strategic planning process will, inevitably, lead to personnel shuffling. You may find that not everyone is meant to follow your plan. Companies cannot afford to have people pulling in alternate directions from the overall vision of the leadership. While this is especially true in tougher economic times, it should be practiced in good times as well.

People need to know where they're going. Simply remember the three Rs as the key to making a strategic planning process live in your company: reviewing, refining, and repeating the plan, all in a timely fashion. Sharing the message and vision is the leader's job, but just saying it will be so does not make it happen. Implementation of the tactical and practical "how to" components is what makes the strategic plan come to life and allows your goals to be more than mere dreams.

People like to see activity happening around them. But sometimes activity can be confused for productivity. They are not the same. Pedaling a bike with a flat tire requires a lot of activity, but it isn't very productive to get down the road. If we do not take the time to think and plan out our work, we actually increase the necessary activity (and possibly the wrong activity) required to perform our duties. Organizing our work into a plan allows us to review the steps we think we should take and then adjust them before committing more time and energy down a frustrating path.

When you hit bumps in the road—look back on them,
take those lessons to heart, and learn.

Throughout life, we are tested by what we're going through. My philosophy includes looking back as well as planning for the future. Although we aren't given the ability to look, step-by-step, into the future with absolute certainty, we do have the ability to use our own rearview mirror to see where we have been and what we have come through. If you stop and look back, you can connect the dots of where God led you during the tough times when you wondered why you were in those situations. You can see the value in those experiences. It might be tempting to always try to look ahead, but if you saw only the problems and pitfalls of a possible future, you might lack the courage and faith you need to move forward. When you hit bumps in the road—look back on them, take those lessons to heart, and learn. That's how we can make changes to our futures.

It has been my experience that when a business goes to market the right way, the community responds by supporting that company. This is not to say that people will pay any price to do business with you, but they do look at the value equation and, more often than not, want to do business with companies that model their desired traits.

The days when companies had decades to learn from mistakes are long gone, replaced by split-second decisions that can make or break a company's image overnight. Solid ethics and business basics in the boardroom, combined with integrity at home, is what allows executives to find footing on the shaky foundation that is the modern business age. Even with all the tools at the disposal of a conscientious executive, mistakes happen. How you recover and learn from them is what separates average from excellent.

Leadership Heartbeats

- Practice solution-based customer service. Think bigger than just the customer's immediate need.
- Be true to yourself and your values as you plan your business.
- Embrace dynamic (ongoing) strategic planning.
- Remember: reviewing, refining, and repeating the plan (the three Rs) to make strategic planning live in your company.

CHAPTER 7

MARKETING

"People don't buy what you do;
they buy why you do it."

—SIMON SINEK

Advertising is not the entirety of marketing, but it is one tool in your marketing toolbox. Marketing includes everything that the public sees about your business: advertising, public relations, even the name. This could include branding on the vehicles that support the company, any place your logo appears (from business cards to billboards), and printed ads or radio or television commercials. These are all tools that you can utilize at differing levels depending on how you want to influence the market.

Just as people are quick to judge other people by first

impressions, so they will judge your company. Therefore, you want to send the right message in a very consistent way that is quickly recognized and that elicits the reaction you desire. Of course, your team members have to back up the impression with their execution, but the first step is to get people interested in doing business with you. Think of the message as a person's clothes; they create the very first impression that sets the tone for the rest of the conversation. I believe this is where investing heartbeats is well worth the time it takes to define and refine your specific message.

Marketing is how you are seen in the marketplace.

You can turn on or off, ramp up or ramp down advertising through the amount of money you spend, but you can never turn off the marketing. Marketing is how you are seen in the marketplace. It is your own identity connected to the brand and that of your company or your product or service. This is why a set of guiding principles is so important: What you stand for defines your brand.

What's in a name?

Naming a business is part of marketing, but it's also part of the equation for how profitable a company will be in the future. I see a lot of people in my industry and others who have a strong desire to put their name on their company. I advise people to be very careful about doing that, because when you decide to exit—as someday you eventually must—a company with your name—named after a single person—will always be perceived as you. That is a difficult hurdle to get over if you want the business to have longevity. This is especially true in smaller companies that focus on personal services, such as the trades, but it can be a problem in larger firms as well if the company name is solely centered on a particularly charismatic personality.

You have to intentionally build transferable value as you go through the company's life—and in that, no one person is solely responsible for the value of the company. The ideal company has great people in it and really good processes; great companies are process driven, not personality driven, and have high-quality products or services. Consider a name for a business that is easily identifiable with the service or product you are providing.

If you've purchased a company or are making major changes to an existing business, you may be tempted to change the name. However, changing the name or brand identity of an established business can be treacherous territory. Your company name is what you stand for. You lose recognition value and may lose your current customer base if the name change means people are no longer familiar with the company. You absolutely risk people thinking you are out of business if you make a change for change's sake. Only if the brand has a bad reputation should you change it.

When I came to Conditioned Air, I did not like the light blue, red, and black lettering. But when I found out how long it had been that way, that it was highly recognizable by the public, and that the company had a good reputation, I wasn't about to change it—the font, the style on our trucks, anything—no matter how much it didn't suit my own personal preferences.

It was my job to make sure everything—all instances of our logo and brand—was consistent even though I didn't love it. I learned early on in my business career that changing something just to change it is not good, especially when it is a publicly recognized brand. Never take the value of a brand lightly, and be slow to change branding when the public has already accepted and embraced it. All logos, letterhead, business cards, and so on should be in alignment with each other.

One or two words—the name of the company, the name of an organization or a product—immediately conjure up a paragraph inside your mind that you subconsciously run through. Your customers also have this experience about your brand. Say the words "Holiday Inn" or "Ritz-Carlton," and you're already past the point of analyzing which is which. Both say loud and clear, "This is our name, and this is what you get." The value of your company is what you make of that brand. If you have the ability to put your personal feelings about how you name things or name companies aside, you're ahead of the pack, because it is going to take a long time for people to understand your business in general. A business owner who wants to name his business after himself should expect issues down the road if he goes to sell it or transition it—especially if it is built around one person.

Most Conditioned Air customers don't know me personally, but they know the technicians who show up at the door. The value they get goes back to what we stand for. That's far more important than a name. Even when I do our advertisements, I really try to keep my ego in check. I don't use my title or throw my weight around. I simply say, "Hi, I'm Theo Etzel, with Conditioned Air."

This also factors into the economics of the company in marketing expenses. Should you rebrand the company when it was named after someone? Every situation is different. Be aware that you'll live with whatever the consequences of such decisions are financially and in the marketplace.

Advertising

The basics of your message really should be at the heart of your business. But what is that, exactly? And how do you find it? And once you do, how do you incorporate traditional and unorthodox methods to share that message with your customers?

Traditional methods of advertising require that the message be very succinct, in that you just don't have much time to get a message out. So I have chosen to focus on the *how* and *why* we do what we do rather than simply what we do. I am looking to communicate uniqueness in our business and industry and want to place those values up front in our messages. You must determine exactly what bullet points are critical to communicate for you and your audience.

As you expand into the newer tools in marketing and advertising, you have the opportunity to tell a more detailed story if you can get people to visit your web page and read and see examples of your company's character. This is where you can expand on those bullet points and add more color to the picture you wish to paint for people. In any form of communication, the message must be relevant to your audience members and must hit some emotional buttons to compel them to listen to it. Just because you are telling it, doesn't mean people will listen. If you are uncomfortable determining the message and the audience appeal, you may need to seek the help of a professional in the marketing and advertising field to home in on the key points to promote.

> *The message must be relevant to your audience members and must hit some emotional buttons to compel them to listen to it.*

Take commercials. Many CEOs and business owners elect to record their own commercials, and I am one of them. I happen to enjoy doing the commercials and enjoy writing them, but I also began my career in radio—announcing sports in high school. This means I am very comfortable on air. My ability to speak comes naturally to me, and I'm recognized in the community for my voice more than for my face. Even in line in the grocery store, people recognize my voice from our commercials and compliment us on our style of advertising, because it is straightforward and doesn't come off as gimmicky or cheesy.

The style of the ad and the message you're communicating is the heart of the matter. I've been a big part of the brand, but it doesn't have to be me. At some point, that will stop, because the time will come when I won't be able to record ads for the company. That's why the company must be bigger than the spokesperson communicating the message.

Challenges often arise, to the detriment of the company, when ego comes into play. There are a lot of people who don't need to do their own radio or TV ads. If you are at all uncomfortable speaking on camera or on air or posing for a photo in a print ad—or even unsure of your writing skills in an advertorial—then don't do it. Doing your own ads is not the most important thing; you can ask someone else in the company or hire professionals to do the actual speaking.

However, it is part of your job to determine the direction you want the advertising to go. Do you want it to be educational? Promotional? Off the wall? Comedic? Do you want to have a character in the ad? I chose to do something that is very straightforward, that communicates how and why we do what we do—not even so much *what* we do. We found this approach to be very effective and to resonate well with the customers in our industry.

The modern term for this is *content marketing*, and it ties in with information and websites or a blog—but we try to have content inside the ad conveying a message that compels people to do business with us.

This is important for several reasons. For example, if you're in a business that deals with consumers and have bad competition—companies in the same business who don't complete things to standards or who are not truthful about who they are in the marketplace—it actually hurts your company as well. The buying public becomes distrustful, and even companies with high standards can get lumped in with the reputation of a tarnished industry or competition. We often find ourselves in the education process, differentiating ourselves from the competition through communicating how and why we conduct business as we do. This is part of gaining the consumer's trust.

DIY advertising versus hiring an agency

Until my ad budget at Conditioned Air shot north of $200,000, I was able to control our advertising and manage it myself, to a degree. But as that number grew, it became a major time and research investment—between meetings with account representatives for all the different venues and tracking, it got to be too much for me. What I was not good at was determining or seeing an extended marketing plan for the year. I had some of those pieces put in place, but other things arose, and it was more scattered than I wanted it to be.

To rein in our advertising and to become more intentional, I sought out professionals to help me map it out. I am still involved in it, but I consider their recommendations. We work together, typically in the fall, as they put a proposal together for the following year. We determine the budget, which now exceeds a half a million dollars. We put that together, but then they give me a plan for an entire year. I still write my own scripts and record my own radio ads, but we enlist professionals to help us with the video and all the planning.

The money we spend on an agency is a wash. Yes, we have to pay them based on what we spend. But the agency gets a discount, and they help with the creative process. They also save me a great deal of time: When I do a commercial, I simply email it to the agency, and they handle it from there. In employing the services of an accomplished agency, you get professionalism and credibility. Just as you want people to hire you because you're an expert in your area, you have to instill that trust in experts to help with advertising. For us, it is well worth the expenditure.

Vetting an advertising agency is a huge ordeal. Here are my top tips for vetting and understanding the process of working with an agency:

- It is an interview process. Once you find agencies that pique your interest, sit down and interview someone you might be working with at the agency to see whether you are both on the same page.

- Without a somewhat significant budget, you may not get a great response. Pay attention to the ads you see on TV or hear on the radio. You can tell which ones were willing to spend. Budgeting for the ad not only allows the agency to create something more polished, but it also indicates to the audience that you are successful, which instills confidence in your brand.

- Keep watch for ads that get your attention. If you happen to see something you actually like, don't be afraid to ask which agency did the ad. They may be able to do something that will catch your customers' attention as this ad did yours.

- Don't fall into the trap of believing everyone will respond to the same things you respond to in an ad. Be willing to stretch your faith. At the end of the day, you must be pleased and proud of what you're putting out there for the public.

- Use the same adage to interview an ad agency that you use in your own company: Does the agency have integrity and is there truth and trust?

- Use people you know and respect. I had been exposed to our ad agency and was very pleased with their work doing smaller projects. We meshed well, and loyalty plays a role in such situations for me, so I let them try some larger projects for us. Consequently, we have been doing business together for seventeen or eighteen years, which is uncommon in the advertising business.

Choose an agency that's willing to do just as good of a job on the smaller jobs as the larger ones. Those efforts helped the agency land our bigger work.

- Make sure you like working with your agency. It comes down to quality people: Our agency reps are extremely gracious and very responsive, which certainly adds to the quality of my life and the success of the company.

What kind of advertising to use

When choosing which advertising package to use, look for frequency and reach. Advertise to reach your target audience: What percentage of the market are you actually reaching? The deeper, the better. Make sure to ask your agency to report how many times you are getting exposed to that target audience. Marketing and advertising is a long-term investment. You can't do it for a couple of weeks and step back to examine the results; you have to look at it after it's had time to simmer.

We started out on a relatively small budget: $20,000 to $30,000. I looked for the best value I could in this price range. At that time, it tended to be zoned cable TV. I could target the zip codes in areas of town where we could make the biggest impact. Today, the landscape is ever changing with the emergence of social media. So, depending on your product or service, there may be limited or extensive social media avenues to explore. At Conditioned Air, we are evolving as well while still using traditional methods.

Timing your advertising

Timing is critical. I time our advertising seasonally, which tends to be the way our business works: We advertise more often during the times of the year when people need their air conditioning maintained. After all, how many people are thinking about HVAC when they are running around wrapping Christmas presents? Until I figure out how to make someone want to wrap up a condenser in a big red bow, it doesn't do me much good to advertise around the holidays.

I learned this the hard way, by doing it wrong in the ice cream business. Several years ago, in my Atlanta-based ice cream business, I used targeted cable ads. In the summertime, we had a line out the door. I thought, mistakenly, that it's better to advertise in the winter, when people aren't thinking about ice cream. What I learned is that people who will come in for ice cream when it is 40 degrees outside will do so whether there is an ad or not, and people who will not eat ice cream when it is below 80 degrees don't patronize the business in the winter simply because of an ad. Those ads made no difference; I was advertising to an empty audience.

I also realized that if I ran two-for-one brownie sundaes between 5:00 p.m. and 7:00 p.m., I probably would not sell a lot of ice cream. Families are not likely to change their dinnertime habits for discounted ice cream. And if you want people to come in after dinner, don't put strings on it—make the special for any time they want it. It's about the customer's convenience, not yours.

You can't change societal habits
based on a coupon or an ad.

A guy in the hardware store where I used to shop taught me this lesson about making mistakes in advertising: He used to advertise garden hoses on Tuesday because that was the slowest day in the store. But then he decided to run that ad on a Saturday, when people are doing projects at home and in the yard. This drew people in, and he sold more hoses. You can't change societal habits based on a coupon or an ad.

In my ice cream business, I switched my ad schedule to begin at the end of winter and run into spring, because I wanted people to think of my store when they wanted to go out for ice cream, and it worked. When they wanted ice cream, they remembered our ads and came in. So now in the air conditioning industry, even though we do advertise year-round, we ramp up and ramp down based on the season, concentrating on the period just before we think they'll need the product—late spring and into the summer.

The value of loyalty and customer service

Loyalty breeds loyalty, and that is another way my ad agency impressed me. I had established relationships with ad reps at these various media outlets. The agency kept and honored those relationships. I seek to protect people when I can, which breeds loyalty. To this day, those reps throw bones my way in the form of little fire sales or ads that have opened up on major sports events. I've made some strategic last-minute buys that way. And you know what? We have a very good understanding. I get back to them fast—whether it is a yes or no—and they keep the offers coming.

Be very, very careful of using first-time-customer specials. Many customers—especially long-time, loyal customers—find those repulsive. What those kinds of ads tell me is that while I may have been with a company for eight years, for example, that company clearly cares more about the new guy than me, a loyal customer.

Take cell phone or cable companies. During the first six months, they roll out the red carpet, but after that, they often retract that deal. The same applies when it comes to customer calls: Press 1 for sales, and your call is answered right away. Press 2 for support, and you could be on hold for an eternity. It goes back to the brand you want to be known as—are you the brand that answers the phone and helps customers? If so, everyone at your firm better be on the same page with how you are going to help customers. I always want a person answering the phone. This level of service can help you share the heart of your message in advertising.

Discounts and coupons

Another strategy that's been helpful at Conditioned Air is to make sure you focus on the value of your product and service and not the price. And if at all possible, avoid discounting your product or service. Otherwise you've just told the customer, "Hey, guess what: Our product isn't worth it."

Here's an example of how this type of advertising can wreck a message. A car dealership near my office tells me in ad after ad that the price of their cars is what sells them. In these ads, which may cost thousands of dollars, they say nothing of their service department (do they even have a service department?), what they are selling, or if the warranty on their cars is meaningful. Nothing about "how" they are better than their competition. So in my mind, they have reduced their product to commodity levels and they did it to themselves.

We rarely, if ever, use coupons. We offer a good value at our established price. It is a fair trade of service for dollars. From 2012 to 2014, Conditioned Air went from $28 million to $40 million in revenue. We did not coupon or employ first-time-customer advertising of any kind. We focus on value, and the customer seeks out that value.

Balance in advertising

Some businesses rely on extreme ad tactics. Be careful of this as well. Another car dealership has an owner who insists on doing his own ads. He yells at the camera, would generally be considered off the wall, and gives away cruises and iPads with car sales. Is he recognizable? Yes. He gets high marks for coming in and owning a market for publicity. He has that down. But does it resonate with everyone? Not always in a good way. He has certainly made an impact, and that is his shtick—but that's not necessarily yours or mine.

Many famous ad campaigns for national brands have won awards and are recognizable. Textbooks have been written on those campaigns. But remember: In many cases, that ad campaign hasn't been successful in moving the bar on the product, in actually increasing sales. People remember the ad, not the product. Alka-Seltzer and Volkswagen both experienced this years ago when they had memorable ads, but those ads didn't result in significantly more business.

That's why people began to rethink the content and not the form. There is a balance when it comes to making an ad interesting, meaningful, and—most of all—impactful to the point that your consumer takes action in a positive way toward your product or service.

Public relations: How to make the most of your media

Public relations (PR) is a part of marketing that ties into advertising, but CEOs and business owners all too often want to lump the two together. There is a real art to garnering PR stories in media that highlight things about your personnel or the company overall or a new initiative, market, or new product—whatever it may be—and to getting that information published. In the field of PR, I absolutely believe you have to hire a PR professional. Either that individual will be in your ad firm or you will need to seek out a PR firm or practitioner with excellent ties to your local marketplace. I selected a different firm to handle Conditioned Air's PR, specific to our market, who had local contacts in the media and elsewhere.

The reasoning behind this is that local PR people are planted in your backyard and understand the steps to get media outlets to publish stories about your business. This is different from advertising, which costs you to place it. Media coverage won't cost you anything to publish—except for what you spend on your PR contract with the practitioner. And how local your PR person is really matters when the majority of your customers are within a certain geographical range.

Measuring your marketing: How to know if it's working

At Conditioned Air, we are very deep in the marketplace. So whether you hear us on the radio, see an ad on TV, run across us on the web, see our trucks in the area, or even talk to a neighbor and hear our name, most people know us. Our business is a demand-based business—not a daily basis business. When you need us, you really need us and usually not until then.

So it's part of my job to ensure that our company appears in front of consumers frequently enough and at the proper time to cause them to call us when the need arises. And I would caution people not to be delusional; until your customers need your service or product, they will not be calling. A retired customer is going to go play golf until he needs the AC fixed; we simply need to be on people's radar screen when they need us. The most likely and profitable scenario is when people need your product or service, you're already in their mind, and they call you. You want to be the sole provider of a product or service in the customer's mind when that need arises. You want them to think of only you. That's when you own the market.

Referrals are the ultimate marketplace validation. Let's say someone needs tires or is hungry for cupcakes. Your name needs to be on the tip of their tongue, so they not only come to buy your cupcakes but also talk to their coworkers about them, putting you in that new customer's mind too, thereby locking out the competition. I term it this way: Whatever I do, I want to be adopted by the community so that referral business becomes my number one form of marketing.

Referrals are the ultimate marketplace validation.

Nothing beats a referral. Advertising is expensive, especially if you are not keeping the customers you convince to call you. Talk about wasting dollars! Customer acquisition is the most expensive process there is. If you're just churning people because your processes are lousy, you will constantly have to try to plow new ground. Once they are in the door, keep your customers happy, and they will provide you with more business than you can shake a stick at.

All this said, there are ways to measure marketing impact, and you can employ all sorts of tracking applications, ads run on particular stations or in specific publications—using various phone numbers and such, what zip code something was mailed to—but customers are not always compliant with these methods. This means you have to be very careful when assigning cause and effect to advertising.

Marketing is a big-picture process. There is and always will be some inefficiency in that process. But with a good agency that is more of a trusted partner than just a vendor and a good read on the marketplace, you can determine what is working and what is not.

Some companies employ a "How did you hear about us?" quiz. Sometimes customers will share that information with you, but we are very careful not to quiz people over the phone. Typically, when people call us, it's because they have a problem and are in a hurry to fix it. We don't want to waste their time; we want to get them cool again!

Social media hype

Everyone seems to be hopping on the social media bandwagon. Disruptive advertising is any that interrupts the customer, such as a TV commercial that interrupts a program. Although social media, including Facebook, Pinterest, message boards, and so on, are less disruptive, it's difficult to judge how the audience will react to your ad. People have promoted social media as appropriate for everyone, but I beg to differ. I think it is much better used for either fad-based but trendy products or experiences or services that get a ground swell behind a particular item. For tweeting out the fresh catch of the day, a drink special, what's new on the menu—things of that nature—it's crucial. Those kinds of messages could potentially change people's minds about how they will spend their money that day, because these are more impulse-type items. For example, people might have set plans, but seeing that their favorite restaurant has announced their favorite fish as the catch of the day could cause them to change those plans.

We at Conditioned Air are more of an intentional or demand-based product. Consequently, our tweets and blogs are of a general nature on how to keep an AC system going, maintenance, something of interest from our offices that people can tag to each other, and so on. But even so, you're not going to generate the masses and masses of people that you need in our business via social media. We have to be in front of consumers when they need us. Therefore, we use a combination of media, but we spend more on traditional advertising than on social media. We invest in our website and in connectivity because that is an advancing trend. Only you can determine how much or how little of your resources should go toward social media, but weigh carefully how much of your own time as CEO or the owner of your business should be spent there. Make those heartbeats count.

Leadership Heartbeats

- What you stand for defines your brand.
- Make all branding consistent—logos, letterhead, business cards, vehicle signs, and so on.
- Determine what bullet points are critical for your company to communicate.
- Consider hiring an ad agency if your marketing budget is high.
- Advertise to reach your target market.
- Be sure to communicate the *why* of what you do.
- Pay attention to the timing (e.g., seasonal, time of day) of your advertising.
- Focus on the value of your product or service and not on the price.
- Utilize public relations to make the most of your media.
- Consider whether social media is appropriate for your business-marketing plan.

CHAPTER 8

RUNNING A BUSINESS

*"He that waits on fortune is
never sure of a dinner."*

—BENJAMIN FRANKLIN

In the game of business, your profit and loss (P&L) statement is your scorecard. As a leader, you had better know how to read that scorecard. Could you imagine being a coach and not being able to read a scoreboard? How would you know which plays to make? I know people who don't read their scorecards for a year, and—trust me—businesses can get way off track in that time. You as the CEO or owner should have a very good understanding of the financials. If that is not your strong suit, take courses to learn more.

The leader of an organization needs to understand what is

involved in all aspects of the company. This doesn't mean they have to be able to perform all the jobs required, but you have to understand what is involved—especially the financials.

Part of your role as the leader of your organization is to ensure everyone knows how to read the scorecard. Employees need to know what's important and what's not so that they know which parts of their job to focus on. It also allows them to see the big picture of the business and all that goes into its operation and the impact each person has on the success or failure of the organization. That requires spending time with your team and sharing your skills. Here are a few skills and habits that leaders often possess that are critical in the business world:

- A strong grounding of values in right and wrong
- Perseverance
- An attitude of gratitude
- An understanding of the value of money
- A strong focus on communication, writing, and language
- Curiosity
- Advanced financial skills
- Interpersonal relationship skills
- An understanding of economic influences and free enterprise
- The ability to speak in front of people

All of these skills are helpful, but at the top of the list of actions that lead to continued success, I would place tracking your business's profitability. Look to the future, and see possible trends in your business. Predicting problems allows you to be reactive and nimble, so it is important to be responsive in your business, especially when the market changes.

A common mistake I see businesses make is producing a P&L sheet but ignoring a balance sheet. The P&L is a *result* of producing a balance sheet; you must have both, but the real knowledge of how the money is made comes off of the accounts posted on the balance sheet.

Because doing an accurate balance sheet requires attention to detail and some extra work, if you don't want to take inventory or invest in a real-time inventory system, you're really not going to know what your cost of goods is and where that inventory goes. Guessing at your cost of goods because you were guessing at your inventory results in an unknown bottom line.

In-house or outsourced finances?

Having an in-house CFO is ideal if you're able to do so. But there are two functions that are critical to outsource if you can't afford or aren't ready to hire an in-house CFO. Those would be (1) legal and (2) accountancy and tax preparation—especially when you are a small business. The accounting rules and tax laws change so often that you really should rely on a specialist to prepare those for you. Hiring outside sources for those functions allows you to focus on what you do best, and, in turn, you are able to rely on hired professionals to do what they do best.

An in-house bookkeeper or comptroller will keep the accounts straight for the business, including accounts payable and receivable. Typically, bookkeepers or comptrollers will not be able to prepare taxes or know the current laws, but they can do the heavy lifting of the accounting side by preparing the books. At the very least, pay an accountant to read a balance sheet and P&L and become familiar with those documents. If you are trying to hire people in an accounting department, let the outside accountant interview them for expertise and qualifications before you interview them for culture and fit. If you don't know the right questions to ask, get someone to help you who does.

The comptroller comes into play after the bookkeeper, and people in this role will know the nuances of accounting rules—how to book revenue, when to recognize it, when to recognize expenses and amortization schedules, and other more complicated financials. You need someone like that to guide you through the legality, all the rules, and what is best in your particular industry. In contrast, your bookkeeper is an entry-level accounting position, and the person in this role should know the rudimentary accounts to place expenses or receipts in.

When you are able to hire one, your CFO will oversee everything, including the accuracy and timely distribution of the numbers. Technically, the CFO has authority over everyone in the company regarding financial reporting responsibilities. CFOs trump everyone in that realm because they are responsible for tracking profit and loss. Their names are on a lot of documents, and they are assigned a lot of accountability and responsibility.

Find a qualified person who will be responsible
for accurate numbers in your business.

As in anything that requires expertise, whether your company needs a bookkeeper or you can afford a true CFO, find a qualified person who will be responsible for accurate numbers in your business. A person of utmost character is essential. I have been fortunate to be able to hire a very qualified CFO who is not afraid to point out problem areas, red flags, and warning signs for us to react to. Our CFO has decades of experience, which has enabled her to become a tremendous asset in every facet of the company. She is an integral part of the leadership team and a partner in the business. Her insights are key to the strategic planning process and budget development.

Although I am a person who does know the nuances of financial records, I am not well versed in the mechanics of accounting. I need professional assistance to make sure all the numbers are properly accounted for. This also allows me to focus on other areas of the business in the creative and strategic and implementation side of the work we do.

When we first started the company, we just gathered our

numbers and handed them off to an outside party, and then we had a comptroller. Later, we had one person acting as COO and CFO, but then came the time when the two positions needed to be pulled apart. I knew it was time to reach out and hire a CFO when we hit a threshold. The truth about a profitable company is revealed in accurate numbers. That is your scorecard, but there is a human element to the financial side of a business as well. No one knows the details better than the person in that role.

Calculating the actual cost of business

Don't try to compete in the marketplace on price alone. Learn what it takes to sell value in your product. In my case, what does it cost me to provide service at your house? I need to know all the various inputs, what benefit packages are included in paying the serviceperson, the cost of a vehicle and its wear and tear, insurance, the cost of having a truck stocked with rolling inventory. All these costs must get allocated. What do I have to charge to get a fair return on that process? Then all that has to be weighed against what the market would allow me to charge for the value that I bring.

The marketplace doesn't pay for inflated costs and inefficiencies inside my business if we simply choose to be lazy about how we perform our tasks. As it says in Ecclesiastes 10:18, "If a man is lazy, the rafters sag; if his hands are idle, the house leaks." We will cease being the preferred company if we don't pay attention to the details. People vote with their dollars, and again, if the value isn't there, they stop voting.

Use caution when overextending credit to "buy" business— if that doesn't convert into cash in a timely manner, you can get into big trouble.

Predicting economics

In the grand scheme of economics, remember that bad times never last forever, and neither do good times. We are always in a state of flux. We find ourselves growing, trying to maintain where we are, or dealing with declining sales or a shifting market. Being proactive in the anticipation of these changes, being diversified in the marketplace, having the courage to implement your plans, and leading your organization to quickly react and adapt are key elements in being proactive in changing market conditions.

My crystal ball is somewhat muddy at times. Predicting the future is out of my hands, and predicting the exact timing of events is even further removed. However, I am a big believer in looking out as far as is practical with economic information that tends to be a leading indicator for your industry or company. We all have internal leading indicators that tell us something about our customers and their spending habits.

One technique known as *trending* can help you track your company's profits. You can measure whether you are increasing or decreasing in certain areas of the business. If you are decreasing, what do you need to do to adjust how you are doing? We constantly look at how things are going to improve our performance and behavior in the marketplace. This will vary from business to business, but for us, it may be new products or technologies that we need to incorporate to stay current with consumer demands.

We can accomplish this by plotting revenues and profits by month and comparing the percentage increase or decrease on a graph. To reduce seasonality—or even negate it—you can use a trailing three-month total and a trailing twelve-month total. This will allow for a clearer picture of your real progress. It will give you a visual of the direction of the company's results. This allows you to track your *rate of change* and not just the actual value of the change. Is the *rate* increasing, showing positive growth? Or are you increasing at a decreasing rate? Or, worse, are you decreasing at an increasing rate? My friends at the Institute for Trend Research, in New Hampshire, have done extensive work in this area for me as well as for other businesses, and I highly recommend their expertise.

Predicting economics is a very intentional process. This means being proactive, as opposed to reactive. It must be top of mind for you and the team. It can include brainstorming, discussions, and requests for ideas from all personnel. The understanding of the results is important to the success of the entire company. It allows you to help chart the course for continued success. People in sports need to know the score so they can adjust their play calls to fit the situation. Just as they adjust depending on the score, we need to be able to judge when to take greater risks and when being conservative is the prudent play.

Keeping people in the dark about how the business is going and then issuing a change in course doesn't allow team members to understand the why *of the decision.*

If we don't try to educate or share all the analysis gathered, people will not understand what it takes to run the company and where they fit in. Keeping people in the dark about how the business is going and then issuing a change in course doesn't allow team members to understand the *why* of the decision. You may very well know what needs to be done, but reducing their understanding of the reasons for change makes it look arbitrary and doesn't gain team member buy-in. Change with no reason attached simply looks like "more work for me" from the other side of the conversation.

Here are a few scenarios to consider based on my time at Conditioned Air. When repair tickets are increasing on older equipment, replacements may be in for a decline in the near term. It shows us that people are willing to put less expensive Band-Aids on a problem rather than investing in a true fix or solution. They are, in essence, buying time or time-shifting their purchase decision.

Are more people financing purchases? That could indicate that cash is getting tight or that the customers' confidence in their employment is questionable and that they are holding on to cash.

To plan for your economic future, it's important to see further than just trends that develop. Look outside local patterns and really focus on leading economic indicators.

As I said a few paragraphs before, for our trending, I've relied on an outside firm, the Institute for Trend Research (www.ITReconomics.com), out of New Hampshire. With an excellent track record for looking at trends of such things as the Purchasing Managers' Index, construction spending in various categories, money supply, corporate bond rates, and so on, they accurately predicted the recessionary trend for 2009 and recovery in late 2010. They also provide industry cycle stages and help interpret the data for easier digestion and use. Positioning yourself properly by anticipating a changing economy is a decided advantage over the competition. This concept, of course, goes for good and bad times equally. Looking for upcoming trends with the use of economic data can let you see what's coming in the future.

Watch for more advance warning and respond to that data with a plan, which will result in fewer casualties in employees and will reduce your own stress levels. When you do call for a change in course, commit and educate people as to why the change is needed. Being able to start early on this new plan is ideal. If you've waited too long and don't have the luxury of time, quick, decisive action is needed if you are to save the company.

You must use the information you receive from your trending report to reposition your business in advance of the market shift you see coming. For example, if you're heavily into construction but light in service and you see the slowing of construction coming, shift assets and resources to the service side. This could significantly improve your chances of surviving a construction market slowdown. But doing so ahead of time is the key. Once the economic wave has hit, it's too late.

Relying solely on new construction for income and profit makes you vulnerable to wide swings in that industry. Having a well-balanced company, with multiple profit centers (retail, service, contracts, construction), can help smooth out the peaks and valleys in the economy in each specific area. For the most part, not all areas of your business will be at the top or bottom at the same time. While this may limit your potential income one year, it may help you avoid massive losses the next. Spreading out risk and your resulting reward level depends on your risk tolerance.

John Kotter and Holger Rathgeber's book *Our Iceberg Is Melting* (St. Martin's Press, 2006) goes into further detail about quick change and practical advice on accomplishing this mission.

How to handle decline and growth

Because many of us will at some point experience a downturn in overall business, we should make it a habit to look at overhead costs. I break items down into needs and wants when we discuss this in our weekly management meetings. Frankly, a consistent review of needs versus wants in all economic cycles is the best approach to avoid overspending when incomes are up.

You are not going to save your way out of declining sales. You must be able to grow your business to remain successful. If you notice sales decreasing, you must react to that and take action, including reducing overhead and determining why sales are declining. This is the time to have all hands on deck looking at how to increase sales.

Sometimes the needed action may seem counterintuitive to the circumstances. For example, when sales started sliding in 2008, we accelerated our advertising and increased what we spent on all our marketing efforts to capture extra market share. I noticed many of our competitors pulling back and thought the time was right to push and take that risk. It might not have worked, but it did. We were able to stop the slide and actually turn it into a growth mode over the following years.

We were also able to increase the actual area we served by establishing a branch office in another community about a hundred miles north of our headquarters. We did this organically, but you may consider acquisitions as another way to increase sales and gain market share. Of course, new products in your mix are possible if they can be brought to market quickly and you have the expertise to deal with them. Asking your sales staff what customers really want can help focus your team's efforts in a positive way and make a faster impact on the financial success of the organization.

If the pie is shrinking, then you must get
a bigger piece of that pie.

In a declining market, the opportunity for growth still exists. In this scenario, even staying the same relative to the declining market is a win. The opportunity for growth lies in increasing your market share. If the pie is shrinking, then you must get a bigger piece of that pie. Most people pull into their shell like a turtle when a downturn strikes, but stretching your neck out and being bold is what's called for. So, instead of just surviving through a downturn, you have the opportunity to thrive through one.

Let's shift gears and look at situations in a growing economy. Any slowdown won't last forever, so planning what to do when the tide turns is important. The single greatest temptation in a growing economy and booming business climate is to go after too much business. Former British Prime Minister Benjamin Disraeli (1804–1881) said, "Next to knowing when to seize an opportunity, the most important thing in life is to know when to forego an advantage."[4] The focus and discipline that works in slower times also holds true for the good times. Trying to be all things to all people and touch all kinds of markets is a very tough thing to do. Selectively pruning areas of your business that aren't profitable and focusing on what you do really well is a great plan.

You also have to be able to grow your business through volume. Although cost efficiency is good, you cannot grow your business through cost cutting. The only way to grow is to increase your sales.

Growth can also be cash intensive. You can burn through

cash quickly in an attempt to expand into new locations or areas of the business. This can put a strain on the day-to-day operations. Knowing when to say no is important. This is contrary to the instincts of entrepreneurs, because they look for opportunities to say yes.

When someone has a cash flow issue, in many cases, that is a collection issue. This is caused by not paying attention to getting revenue in the door, and when this happens, you are actually financing whatever you are doing for your customer. Be diligent in keeping track of your collections.

You should also take advantage of any leeway your vendors give you in paying your overhead. I don't advocate stringing vendors along, but if they say you have thirty days to pay, you may want to wait twenty-five days before paying so you can use the cash until then. If you have the luxury and the opportunity to take cash discounts—if you pay within ten days, this is typical in today's interest rate market—that's usually a very good thing to take advantage of. Finally, don't prepay for your equipment if possible. Some of our products are as much as $100,000, and I don't want to prepay for that equipment. We want those funds to come in beforehand to cover those expenses.

Economic fluctuations are the nature of the market. Whether on a national or local scale, the marketplace continues to make us act and react to an ever-changing landscape. Look at the long term in plotting a winning course for the business. Keep market diversity in mind so some of the risk is moderated. Find and develop leading indicators that can help predict what might be

changing in your product mix so you can practice proactive decision making. Involve your people in the decisions; more information is better than less. Map out your strategy and plan to
move assertively to implement that plan. And in all cases, show
a positive attitude; it's contagious. Outlasting, out-surviving, and
even thriving in a down business climate is a great feeling to
have for you and your organization. And, surviving the downturn is the only way we get to play in the upturn.

What to do with profits

Looking at it from the perspective of the owner of a small to
midsized company, in the beginning, most of your eggs are in
that company's basket. Blood, sweat, tears, and money—you
are in it with both feet, making it go. As you become profitable
and take profits out of the company for the owners' benefit,
whoever that might be, there are several avenues you have with
that available capital. As the business owner, you can do any of
the following:

- Reinvest that money back into the company, and most
  people take at least a portion of the profits to do so.
- Find alternative investments. For those who take this
  route, I recommend doing this with the guidance of
  professionals. Through real estate, for example, you
  could end up diversifying that income and wealth
  beyond just the one company that you're running.

- Find ways to diversify the company, such as its products, geographic area, or something that adds value to
  the brand.

You might also have the ability to invest in completely different things—the stock market, wine, art—all of which, when
approached wisely, can broaden your risk profile. It's a way to
hedge your bets.

The time frame of the return on investment will vary from
person to person. But it largely depends on a factor rarely considered when the money begins to flow into the company: your
propensity to buy toys versus investing. Are you using your
money wisely or throwing it away on something frivolous?
Regardless of which path you choose, just remember your eggs
are still in that basket.

Finally, beware of profits masking problems in a business.
Profits solve a lot of ills, but just because you are profitable
doesn't mean you should stop looking for ways to continuously
improve. Otherwise, you'll become complacent. Don't get fat
and happy.

> *"Sluggards do not plow in season; so at*
> *harvest time they look but find nothing."*
>
> PROVERBS 20:4

Things change all the time, and the winning combination
today might not be the winning combination tomorrow, so you

constantly have to ask, "Do we have the right people? Do we have too many people? Are we efficient in the way we deliver our product or service?"

America is a capitalist, market-based economy. This means we can earn a profit, tempered by competitive forces, and grow and shrink as we see fit. You will succeed and fail by your decisions and the timeliness of them. Never forget that as a leader, your number one priority for your company is to earn a profit. This is what enables you to employ people and provide support for their families, purchase goods and services in the local community, share your profits with charitable organizations, and reinvest for the strength of your company.

Competition

Beware of becoming complacent because you're making a profit. In the free enterprise system, once you have established that there is a market—by succeeding in it—you can count on other people trying to outperform you to take your place in that market. That is why the free enterprise system works and why profits are held in check.

Most businesses have a low barrier to entry, and because of this, people will enter your space in the marketplace. There will always be someone who brings a product or service that is (at least in the eyes of the consumer) comparable to what you deliver and at a lower price. That may or may not be the correct price, and that company may or may not last, but while it is there, it dampens your ability to let prices rise as if you had a monopoly on the market.

Pay attention to your competition, but pay more attention to the market and what people want. If you focus too much on the competition and just try to keep up with them, you might find yourself going down a path that you don't want to, and that could be devastating. Be aware of your competitors, but know what your customer wants and likes about your company and keep innovating that delivery method.

Competition is a wonderful thing. We compete in the marketplace. However, competition inside a company is *not* a great thing. Some companies want to see that, but it is troublesome. Companies should be a team on the inside and competitive on the outside. Internal competition is detrimental because it can cause the customer to lose at the end of the day.

The marketplace won't pay for your inefficient operation with higher prices when your competition can do it better and for less money.

Part of taking Conditioned Air to such extreme heights had to do with acceptance that life and business are anything but fair. If everyone wanted everything to be fair all the time, why wouldn't the winning team of the Super Bowl go ahead and hand the other team enough points to make it a tie so everyone would go home equal? Clearly, that's not workable—nor is it reasonable that everything in business is, or even should be, fair. One of the reasons people love sports is because there are winners and losers. If you don't care whether you win or lose, don't go into business. You will just waste time and money.

The marketplace won't pay for your inefficient operation with higher prices when your competition can do it better and for less money. Good competition should help us become better and sharper.

My father once told me about General Patton not sitting behind the lines—his Jeep was headed up with the others, and he was willing to be right beside them and go into battle. A leader can never run. Patton also hated defensive positions, because, to him, a retreating position was, in fact, the beginning of defeat.

In business, I personally continue to look at how we maintain an offensive position rather than a defensive position. For this reason, I stay less concerned with my competitors.

I don't want to say, "We made it to the top, boys; that's enough." I want to build the mountain and climb higher. We turned the economic downturn into an offensive. Sure, we had to adjust, but we were going to outrun and outmaneuver. Great companies are called to be better than their competition, and that is a critical part of leadership.

Your exit strategy

For the owner of a business, your major payoff is at the exit. You're building the wealth of the brand to sell to another buyer.

You deserve to be paid for that if you've done it right. Entrepreneurs also look at exit strategies from the very beginning of the business—especially serial entrepreneurs. They are already thinking: *What do I need it to look like before I can get out of it and move on to the next thing I want to do? What does the exit strategy look like down the road? Could there be an outside buyer? Could I sell it to the employees? Could family members take over?*

And for business owners who are appalled I'd even suggest you ever leave your beloved company, news flash: There will be a time in your life when you want to step away. And there may come a time when you *have* to step away. Preparing your company for the time when you are no longer at the helm is just as important as being in charge.

This will sound like the simplest advice ever, but it's also among the most valuable: Write it down. CEOs with nothing written down about the company's processes, how things are done, or sales practices, for example, won't have much of a company to sell if they choose that exit strategy. Your company's processes have to be written down and duplicable, so someone coming in from outside can take over in a seamless transition.

I encourage readers to also read the book *The E-Myth: Why Most Small Businesses Don't Work and What to Do About It* by Michael E. Gerber (HarperBusiness, 1990). The gist of this good read is that you want your company to be franchisable. It should be a scenario where you could give me the playbook, and I could come in and run the company. Work on the systems that are key to your business.

A sound exit strategy and a plan for succession are a critical part of the economics of your business. But it's not just about preparing the business for your exit or transfer; you have to prepare yourself, too. You don't want to be at the office on Friday and then wake up Monday morning, look at yourself, and ask, "What do I do now?"

A large part of a CEO's identity is wrapped up in the business. I have friends who rent office space just to have someplace to go. They get their mail sent there, and they read the paper there, and then they go volunteer for charity or head out to play golf or go boating or whatever.

Prepare both your business and yourself for your eventual exit. Make sure the business can go on without you, but also make sure you can go on without the business.

Leadership Heartbeats

- Track your profitability.
- Outsource legal, accountancy, and tax preparation unless you're an expert and have time to devote to those tasks.
- Calculate the actual cost of business to get a fair return.
- Predicting economics (e.g., trending, tracking rate of change) allows you to chart your business course for continued success.
- Aim to have a well-balanced company with multiple profit centers (e.g., retail, service, contracts, construction).

- Examine overhead costs.
- Plan for growth and declining markets.
- Never forget that, as a leader, your number one priority for your company is to earn a profit.
- Pay attention to your competition, but pay more attention to the market and what people want.
- A sound exit strategy and a plan for succession are critical for the health and well-being of your company.

CHAPTER 9

BEST PRACTICES AND CHANGE

*"Real change only happens when
the pain of where we find ourselves exceeds
the fear of the unknown."*

—THEO ETZEL

In a world where change happens at an increasing speed, mastering the roller coaster that modern business has become is no small feat. Being grounded is the best weapon against getting flung around. If you begin the ride knowing who you are and what your values represent, then you'll hang on *and* you might just be able to influence the results and share those benefits with your staff and family.

Vince Lombardi, the late, great Packers coach is often mis-quoted when people say, "Practice makes perfect." The real quote attributed to him is "Practice does not make perfect. Only perfect practice makes perfect." And, while perfection is typically unattainable, putting into action best practices that point us in that direction can be a true game changer in suc-ceeding in our markets and against competition.

The process of finding, reviewing, developing, and imple-menting best practices for a business is just that—a process. The first question you must ask is "Is it worth the time, risk, investment, and effort to put this process into motion?" If you can answer this question with a yes, then you have begun to answer why you believe it to be important for the company. One lesson every business learned in the recent (and current) economic downturn is that customers are harder to get and keep, and they expect businesses to deliver their goods and ser-vices in as efficient and cost-saving a manner as possible, deliv-ering the greatest value. Aiming to be mediocre is, in reality, giving up on the business. Continuous improvement and striv-ing to be the best in your market is the only road to surviving and thriving in any economic landscape.

If we only look down when we walk, we will surely miss other, and possibly better, paths to our destination.

Many leaders in businesses are taking on more and more daily responsibilities because staff has been cut and there's a more frequent need to look inward. While more attention to detail is a good thing, and very necessary, it can also limit the creativity and choices that are available to us. If we only look down when we walk, we will surely miss other, and possibly better, paths to our destination. Examining alternate methods and programs for the company produces choices that should be weighed against the status quo and in keeping with the company goals.

Looking inward is the first step to being able to look outward. Observing current procedures and asking how we can improve them, even if it is just one or two aspects of that system, sets the pursuit of best practices in motion. Ask your staff to review how they do certain things in their daily work life. Have outsiders come in and observe your operation. Different perspectives bring a whole host of different views, questions, and comments.

Networking for best practices

It's easy to put people within an industry in the same room and have them find many common subjects on which to speak. This also happens to be true of business leaders from diverse backgrounds and a variety of industries. There are more similarities of experiences and challenges in business than there are differences. Just describe a situation (try personnel for a quick response) and then ask the question "Has anyone else had to deal with that?" Most people have had experience with whatever you've described, or something so close as to be applicable. You begin to hear different ways in which the situation was handled. This leads to the realization that there may be a better way to deal with your particular challenge in the future. Conversely, you may share an idea that other people pick up and use to make an incremental improvement in their business as well.

Industry resources such as management information exchange groups and consultants have "industry eyes" to view your company with, and noncompetitive business leaders in your community can bring alternate points of view that cross industry boundaries. I belong to two groups: one is made up of noncompeting HVAC leaders from across the country and meets twice per year, and the second is a CEO group in my community, again from noncompeting businesses, that meets monthly. Both of these groups are solely dedicated to developing, discussing, sharing, and examining best practices for each other's businesses. I have had members from both groups come in to conduct a complete business review, with very revealing results. I have also reviewed businesses myself to offer constructive suggestions and modifications to their methods. No matter which role I was in, I always came away with new ideas for my own company.

Make no mistake: these reviews (whether as a reviewer or reviewee) caused discomfort. But comfort is typically the partner of mediocrity. Discomfort causes change to occur. I've written before that change for change's sake is ridiculous and disruptive. Change for the purpose of improving the person or company is worthwhile and necessary.

Many times, the best practice that comes out of these meetings is a modification or combination of implemented programs in another company, but finding some other procedure and thinking it will fit in your organization without any tweaking is a bit unrealistic. Your organization is unique, and to get the most out of a contemplated change, it must fit within the basic, good foundation of your company. It is up to you and your people to tailor it to your market, goals, and corporate culture.

Is there an association in your industry that fosters gatherings of noncompeting companies to periodically discuss what works in their businesses? You can gain a lot of insight from other business owners.

Implementing change

Knowing that an area of the business is ripe for change and actually making a change occur are two different things. Having my business reviewed and then filing the papers in the filing cabinet would be a big waste of time for all involved, not to mention expensive. Both of the groups to which I belong hold each member accountable for the changes they have agreed to implement. This is, in itself, a best practice for each of these groups. Being held accountable to your peers is a great motivator. It is the constant nudge to move you out of your comfort zone toward continuous improvement. Fact: Leaders need pushing too. We each act as a mentor to one another.

Being held accountable to your peers is a great motivator.

If you attend a conference or seminar or have a business review and come back with dozens of great ideas, your staff will experience terminal frustration and confusion if you attempt to implement them all at once. You may have caught the passion for change, but they just see all the new work and procedures that will have to be put in place. Prioritizing the ideas you glean from others and methodically putting them into practice is the best way to get those practices adopted. As the best-practices process becomes more routine, the changes tend to become more incremental in nature and not as overwhelming as in the beginning. Properly done, your key people will develop an eye and ear for best practices from the other businesses with which they come in contact. Again, it's up to you and your management team to prioritize new ideas.

Finding and implementing best practices inside your company is all about a continual improvement process. Over time, what was a best practice may no longer be the best. The fundamentals on which a business is built typically don't change rapidly. However, the tools we use to run the business often do change more quickly than we would like to admit. Obviously, technology changes affect all businesses. Another area of change is labor relations with our people. Time has changed the expectations of benefits and the level of engagement of our whole staff. Staying competitive, keeping up, and then getting out in front requires us to constantly look for better ways to run our businesses. The implementation of best practices allows companies to evolve.

Having a very broad view of the business that you are in also helps you see ways to put new ideas into practice. For instance, there aren't many buggy-whip manufacturers left today. If those manufacturers had considered themselves in the propulsion business, focused less on the actual horse and buggy, and realized that the buggy whip happened to be the product that fit the bill at the time, where could they be today? Car engines? Rocket motors? The point is, having a very open mind and always looking for ideas that are better than what you do today will keep you leading the way and not asking what happened or where your business went.

Consultants: A double-edged sword

Consultants usually have a very narrow or special focus that they use to aid you in your business, such as when they see a functional problem they can't solve in your business operations, through examining the processes you use or suggesting a product or service you should be selling or a compensation package you should be using for salesmen.

Beware—consultants don't have to live with their results. You do. If you implement what they say, you're going to deal with the fallout. Consultants always come from somewhere else. They will always have a bias, and they will always want to impose that bias on your business and its operation.

In an effort to justify their existence and their fee, they might recommend a change for the sake of change. What this means is that interviewing a consultant is as important as interviewing an employee. You must do your homework on the consultants by talking with their previous clients. Get multiple referrals, and check their references. Your philosophies must align. This is where your due diligence will be critically important. Good consultants can make a very significant positive impact on your business. With others who are subpar, you'll be lucky if you can control the damage and minimize the losses.

Change is a process: Wash, rinse, repeat

Taking your company to a best-practices level is an intentional decision. It will involve some pain, time, trial and error, personnel adjustments, an open mind, and your discipline to see that ideas are executed and implemented to the point where they become habits. Then, as the shampoo bottle says, wash, rinse, and repeat. Keep the process going, and you'll be the one establishing the best practices for your business, market, and industry, which is an enviable position to be in, in any economy. Customers will reward the best companies with the best compliment they can: They'll spend their hard-earned dollars with you and not the company down the street. Increasing business with the best tools and for all the right reasons seems like a best practice to me.

There is a presumed safety with familiarity, and as things change, you can get comfortable, but it takes a little time. And the faster change comes, the more uncomfortable people get. The more exposed to technology people are, the faster those things change. It used to take an hour to bake a potato. In the mighty microwave, it now takes six minutes—and yet modern man becomes frustrated that it takes six whole minutes. If you find yourself yelling at the microwave, you're on the fast track. The speed at which things can happen results in less prep time, less thought process, and less contemplation— not necessarily a good thing. While this is not a condemnation of rapid change when necessary, those changes should be carefully calculated with research and trust in your gut as support for those changes.

Employee buy-in

Warning: Implementing a best-practices process in your company will mean changes are going to happen. Methods, procedures, and even staff may be turned upside down in this process. If a best-practices culture does not exist in the company today, it will be an uphill battle at first. The biggest enemy of change is the status quo: Some will say, "But we've always done it this way." Explaining why the change is necessary in your company's path to become a market leader is going to be critical to your success. Pursuing best practices will push you and everyone around you. Being open to other ways of doing things opens the door for the process to begin.

Change has to be led. Say you want to implement a new computer program across the company. The analysis shows it's not only warranted but also required if your company is to keep growing. But the staff is really looking at it sideways; they just know it's going to mean more work for them. It means leaving their comfort zone. This is not the time for pushing an agenda, no matter how solid it is. This is the time for empathy. Your staff's viewpoint is different from yours. There is pain in learning a new system, and it's up to you, the leaders, to set the employees up for success.

I once had to lead my company through a major computer change. Honest to goodness, it was totally massive. I enlisted two key people to spearhead this process. We began the process eight months before we pulled the trigger to actually change it over. We did not use dual systems: There was no big toe in the water; people were either in or out. The staff understood that as of a certain date, they would no longer have access to the old system. So we went through the necessary steps and had someone to hold our hands two weeks before and two weeks after the system changeover. One of my employees was famous for saying, "I'm all for it, as long as it looks and performs like the old system." Two weeks after that process, she could hardly remember the old system.

When there is change there will be wailing and gnashing

of teeth, and sometimes—and probably more often than not—implementing best practices requires a change in personnel. Not everyone will share your vision or understand why change needs to occur. The only way to be the best company is to have the best people in their best positions. Mediocre people deliver mediocre results, and people who don't fit with the goals of the company can also hold you back. The hardest realization and the largest hurdle for a leader is to acknowledge the fact that as best practices are put into place not everyone in the company will make it. The discomfort of a failing business must be greater than the comfort of a second-rate business to move the leader to change and seek better—and then best—practices.

Purposeful employees recognize that if they need to be counseled on upcoming changes being made in their department, they will be able to seek help. They understand that their supervisory team is open to another type of counseling—listening to their concerns. You, as the team leader, should want to hear what they believe their purpose is in your company. Even understandable pushback will subside.

Adaptability

In a time when executives must adapt to change in the blink of an eye, leadership is essential to successfully navigate the treacherous landscape of contemporary commerce. The leader of an organization must do so much more than just get everyone on the same path.

*Good leadership is about finding solutions and making
changes that will benefit the company first.*

So you have to be judicious about how you introduce change
into an organization. Change for change's sake—just to shake
the wagon so to speak—is never a good idea. Good leadership
is about finding solutions and making changes that will benefit
the company first. And that can include sacrifices.

The moral of leading your staff through change, even when
it's positive, is that a good leader must persevere. You have to
stay with it as long as you're on the right path. Perseverance
and making decisions quickly is critical—but if you're taking
the wrong road and speeding along, all you'll do is get to the
wrong place faster. A wise person once said, "When you're digging a hole for yourself, the first rule is to stop digging and
then figure a way out."

Leadership Heartbeats

- Finding, reviewing, developing, and implementing best
  practices is a process.
- Meet with other business owners/leaders in your industry and outside your industry to network for information
  and best practices.
- Prioritize the ideas you glean from others and methodically put them into practice to get buy-in from team
  members.

- Consider hiring a consultant, but do your due diligence before you choose.
- Acknowledge that as best practices are put into place not everyone in the company will make the transition.

CHAPTER 10

HIRING THE RIGHT EMPLOYEES

"'Come, follow me,' Jesus said, 'and I
will send you out to fish for people.' At once
they left their nets and followed him."

—MATTHEW 4:19–20

I had to laugh when the government was shut down; they used the term *nonessential people* for the government workers who were furloughed. I would like to take a survey of businesses and ask them how many nonessential people they have on their payroll. To successful businesses, that is a foreign concept. You hire the people you need when you need them. If people are nonessential, they should be trained for an essential role or removed from the company.

A successful team means a successful company.

One of the most important tasks you as a leader will ever undertake is hiring. Make no mistake: Hiring effectively begins with leadership. I like to hire people smarter than me and let them use their skills to soar. A successful team means a successful company.

To uncover detrimental traits in a potential hire—before you hire them—don't be afraid to ask open-ended interview questions. Remember, character first: Who you hire and what they stand for is as important as their particular set of skills. Here are a few examples:

- Tell me the last time you found yourself in a compromising work-related situation.
- Tell me something you struggled over and how you solved the problem.
- If you were asked to lie for a coworker, what would your response be?

Although we may think that references on resumes are only going to say great things about the candidate, that isn't always the case. Be sure to check references and gain some added insight into the individual's behavior. Be sure to ask anyone who came in contact with the prospect while in your building how the prospect behaved. Were they polite, talkative, boastful, or arrogant? Because people do business with *people*, it's important that all members of the team represent you and your brand well.

During the interview, are they excited about being in your company, or is this just to see what's out there? I like to see people with enthusiasm about our company. The better candidates do research first about us and know why they want to be a part of our team. This is their time to tell you why they would be a good fit and what they bring to the organization. At the end of the interview, I like to see people who tell us they really want this opportunity; it's like asking for the sale.

The old adage of "hire slow, fire fast" really holds true. Remember that the person you are considering should be putting on his or her absolute best during the interview. If the best isn't up to your standard during the "dating" stage, it won't be any better after you are married to the employee. Be selective. You can't build an *A* company with *C* players.

Cultural fit

Each organization is a little society in itself, with its own culture, and employees must fit into that culture. That's why it's so important for everyone to be accountable. You can't live in a society and not uphold its rules. Those rules must be consistent, upheld for everyone, even though that may be painful for some people. We have had to let people go that we didn't want to see leave, but they didn't fit with the company. Those are the most painful terminations.

Optimism, for instance, is great, and every leader should be able to deliver a hearty dose of it to staffers. But optimism is not a plan. Although a feeling that you're fortunate is one of several secrets to success, hope and optimism are only important in how you approach a plan; they are not the plan itself. Imagine walking into the boardroom to address your top executives and proclaiming, "Okay, guys, here's the plan: We hope for better days. Let's get to work!"

The reverse, which is equally destructive, is the naysayer leader. Now imagine this as your kickoff statement: "Okay, fellas, I've read all the data, and we've all analyzed it. Here's what we're gonna do, but I doubt it will work."

In the classic children's tale *Winnie-the-Pooh*, the central characters include Eeyore, who constantly sees the world with a negative lens and who is the antithesis of Tigger, who doesn't see a problem—ever. I don't know about you, but in leading my organization, I don't have room for Eeyores. I have room for Tiggers—more specifically, focused Tiggers. A focused Tigger is someone who sees the positive in situations but applies realism to the challenges and opportunities at hand. Their approach is uplifting for the team and raises the optimism of the organization. A defeatist attitude has no place on my team. I don't believe it belongs on yours either.

The employee's fit for the position

When you have trust and open communication, you can have continuous feedback and avoid micromanagement. This means matching the right people and their talents with the right positions in the company. It's making the leap between finding the talent and educating or mentoring them that's challenging.

Perseverance and persistence are important,
but only if you're going in the right direction.

When I hear people say, "He's a really good person; he works so hard," it drives me crazy. I agree with you: He works hard. But he might not be the right person for a job, or he might not be directed properly. Hard work is virtue, but it is not the sole attribute that yields the best results. Perseverance and persistence are important, but only if you're going in the right direction. You can expend a lot of energy, but someone who is working hard in the wrong direction is not productive for the company. The leader of the company has to make sure everyone is being led in the right direction.

People often promote employees into roles that they are not ready for. For instance, on the technical side of air conditioning and repair work, this happens all the time.

A technician's mindset is "I have done what I like to do, got paid for it, and fixed the problem relatively quickly."

As the leader, I come in and say, "He is a great technician" and promote him to service manager. But now the technician has to deal with people, conflict resolution, and leadership training; he has no experience or schooling in any of these areas. So not only have I not done anything to make him successful; I have just set him up for failure. Under the pressure, he quits. He used to be our best technician, but I've lost my best technician, and I don't have a service manager either. This is squarely on me and not on him.

This scenario doesn't mean you can't promote someone to leadership. It does mean you have to invest in them to do that. We use techniques like personality and trait testing to make sure the employees' motivations and personalities will fit into these leadership roles. Most of all, if someone can face conflict and move to resolve it, that is essential.

Hiring employees may be the most important thing you do with your business. You have to make sure you find the right people, that they fit within the company, and that you hire them for the right position. Remember, you can educate people to enhance their skills, but you are stuck with their character. A great technician who lies, cheats, and steals does me a lot of harm. Get people with solid character traits on board, and you'll have a powerful team. Without all these elements, you leave yourself, your new hire, and possibly your business set up for failure.

Leadership Heartbeats

- Hire people who are smarter than you.
- Who you hire and what they stand for is as important as their skill set.
- Hire slow, fire fast.
- Instead of Eeyores, look for focused Tiggers who can see the positive in situations and apply realism to the challenges and opportunities at hand.
- Find the right people, be sure they fit within the company, and hire them for the right position.

CHAPTER 11

MOTIVATING
YOUR EMPLOYEES

"Success is not to be measured by wealth, fame, or power but,
rather, by how far you have come using whatever gifts were given
to you by God. If you can honestly say, 'I did my best every time,
even though failure sometimes seemed imminent,' that is success."

—THE EXECUTIVE COMMITTEE (NOW KNOWN AS VISTAGE)

I've written this statement on the back of a little card that I carry with me everywhere. It continually inspires me. I have found that these points really work to inspire my staff and colleagues, and every day, they help me maintain better leadership skills.

As a leader of your own organization, you may find it necessary to craft your own principle of success. Reminders like these—whether they appear in the form of Post-its on your desktop or calendars with your favorite sayings—are a great way to keep your mind and your team focused.

One of the speakers at a Vistage gathering a long time ago made a critical point that leaders are always on stage. "It's showtime!" he exclaimed, the mantra made famous by Michael Allosso. People are always watching you, how you act, what you say, and whether you follow up your talk with action. You can't say one thing and act another way and expect people to do what you say. Your communication must be in alignment with your policies.

> *You can't say one thing and act another way*
> *and expect people to do what you say.*

Allosso's presentation revolved around the theme "you on your best day." He is a tremendous communicator, and I came to know him through Vistage. He has presented seminars for hundreds of groups and is entertaining—his background in theater a helpful tool. But most important, when he creates shows for companies, he gets to know the company and the people involved. Using this idea, we can develop another way for you to lead your staff to greatness: Know your people and model behaviors you want to see in them.

Look back over your life and think about who influenced you in a positive way. One person who influenced me was James Franklin Miller III (known to all as Jim)—my wife Kim's camp director at Camp Greystone for Girls in western North Carolina. He was extremely positive and always had a smile to share with anybody he met. Positivity isn't the be-all and end-all, but it's a trait that successful leaders have.

Jim was fond of repeating, "As you go through life, no matter your goal, keep your eye upon the doughnut and not upon the hole." That poem dates back to the 1920s and, over the years, has come to be referred to as the "Optimist's Creed." I don't even think Jim knew the origin. He just loved the simple visual image it paints for people. He had a lot of little sayings like this that reflected his outlook on life. As you grow in your leadership role and you surround yourself with the right people, I hope you'll develop your own mantras that help you remain steadfast as a leader. People with such a positive outlook are people who have influence, people I want to work with, and the people you'll enjoy working with as well.

Give people purpose

People want purpose in their lives—a bigger calling than just sitting at a desk eight hours a day before going home to the stresses that await them there. To some degree, part of your job as CEO is to market your company to your staff in a way that answers the question they ask themselves every day: "Why is this purposeful?" Creating a purposeful environment and relating to employees is not a human resources duty; it's a job for top leadership.

What is your purpose in leadership? For me, it's part of my purpose to feel and behave a certain way when my hand hits the doorknob. For starters, I make a point of not trying to intimidate anyone. I'm about transparency—implementing things like open-book management and paying attention to details and processes. How I treat people—being respectful, looking out for staff members, and providing a place to work that's better than what they can find in other companies—creates loyalty. Paint a bigger picture, and people who are looking for purpose—even in a nine-to-five job—will appreciate the work.

In the military, soldiers are not allowed to ask, "Why do I have to run up that hill, Sarge?" The military is dictatorial, and it has to be, but employees don't want to feel like they are being dictated to. This kind of leadership creates a revolving door of high turnover, the worst thing to have at a company. You're not running a military brigade, so the people who work for you and with you will need to understand why you're asking them to do something.

Why do I matter? Why do I count? Why should I do it this way? Did the CEO just randomly come up with a process, or is there some purpose behind it? How does my role fit in with the overall picture? These are questions superstar employees will ask themselves. Help them answer these questions adequately if you want them to really participate in the process. *Where can I help? How can I help?* These are the questions you should be asking them.

In many cases, it is useful for staff members to help develop processes, so that they have a sense of ownership of them. This also helps them understand how they actually do affect customers and why those customers should vote for the company every day with their dollars.

It is also extremely important to show people the results of their efforts. As part of our open-book management process, my staff sees how they affect the company's bottom line and that a part of that bottom line is set aside for them to share in. Feeling important makes a person feel good.

A company is not a box; it's a funnel. We receive money from customers, and when we do things right, there are a few coins at the bottom of the funnel. We put some of those coins back in the company to make the company better for the customer, and we share some with our employees. Of course, the owners and capital risk takers should get a return on their investment. We should be in the business of maximizing the value of the enterprise for the shareholders but tempered with a long-term outlook involving the health of the entire organization and the people there. This is how the system works to benefit everyone, but it only works when the employees are motivated for the good of the company.

Parenting skills applied to leadership

Keeping track of small details that affect your business is so much easier if there are guidelines, rules, and procedures to follow. The skills you learn as a parent can be helpful in leading and motivating your employees: Children want boundaries and structure, and employees want structure too. I would never suggest that you treat employees as if they were children. I am merely pointing out that parenting is a form of managing (very young) people. I believe all of us like to have some direction and structure in which to operate. When processes are too loose, it's hard for the employees to know what they are doing and if they are doing something right. Procedures go a long way toward efficiency—at work and in life in general.

Boundaries and limits tend to sometimes lead people to put up walls, and this really is a balancing act. At the end of the day, I'm not going to let lawyers dictate that I can't hug people when their loved one has passed away, for example, but at the same time, I'm smart enough to have glass windows in all office doors, so that there can be no question of impropriety.

A personal set of principles is helpful in delineating boundaries. I believe that the Bible is not just one big rule book; it is God setting boundaries of acceptable behavior. Knowing where those boundaries are allows us to lead a free and fulfilling life.

Barbara Coloroso, author of multiple bestsellers on parenting and child psychology, recommends giving children the responsibility of making appropriate decisions but training them how to make those decisions and how to determine what is appropriate. It's your job to set the boundaries; I wouldn't ask three-year-olds whether they want to go to bed. However, you can ask what they want to wear to bed. They may choose a purple top and green plaid bottoms; it doesn't matter. Allowing them to make the decision is more important than the outcome; these are skills that will develop over time. Small choices will lead to better, bigger decisions because you've exposed them to a decision-making process.

I look to my children to illustrate this philosophy. Kim and I gave our children two choices when it came time for them to drive. We said, "You can get your mom's hand-me-down car when your mom gets a new car, or you can take some of your money and buy your own. But no one will drop a brand new car in your lap."

Our son Chad composes music. He opted to take the minivan to carry his instruments to his after-school job, performing at weddings and funerals. Chad chose to take Kim's car, and our daughter chose to spend some of her savings and bought her car on eBay. My kids learned the same lessons that were instilled in me. I ended up getting a new car, and we helped our kids get their cars, but it was a progression.

Small choices will lead to better, bigger decisions because
you've exposed them to a decision-making process.

Employees require supervision, but there is a balance between micromanaging them and allowing them complete freedom. They need to be allowed to make choices. As a leader, you must establish boundaries inside which the employees can make the choices that are acceptable to you and that are best for the company. This is one of your major responsibilities—the establishment and enforcement of those boundaries. All people—regardless of their age or stage in life—want to know where the boundary is. If this line is made clear to employees, they don't have to second-guess whether they are close to crossing it.

Leadership Heartbeats

- Craft your own principle or mantra of success.
- Align your communication with your policies.
- Paint a bigger picture for team members so they understand the purpose behind the work.
- Set boundaries for your team members, but avoid micromanaging.
- Show team members the results of their efforts.

CHAPTER 12

EMPLOYEE RETENTION

*"The first responsibility of a leader is
to define reality. The last is to say thank you.
In between, the leader is a servant."*

—MAX DE PREE, FORMER CEO

OF HERMAN MILLER

As I mentioned in the last chapter, it is important to avoid employee turnover. For starters, it is very expensive. You have to rehire, which entails the time and monetary cost of creating job ads and interviewing, and you have to retrain, which also costs time and money. You want to reduce that as much as possible with the programs and policies you have in place by creating a good work environment. And that's not always about the money. Trust and pride, ownership, and accountability—people want to show they can do their jobs well, but they need other incentives as well.

Companies need to be nimble and responsive to the external customer and to the internal employees. After all, you're in business, so you can't give away the farm. There is work to be done. But you do have to create an environment where people enjoy being there so you don't run yourself thin on employees and passion.

What employees want out of their work lives has changed dramatically over the past several years. They have to earn a living, but time is now equal currency to a paycheck. For instance, in the HVAC industry, it was common practice years ago to not allow anyone to take vacation in the summer (in the South), because that was the busiest time of year. Today, I know we would not be able to recruit any people to our company if we still tried to have this policy in effect. We have had to alter our staffing matrix over time to accommodate the competitive marketplace for good people.

Previous generations lived to work,
and the newer ones work to live.

The newest and emerging generations of the workforce approach work as a means to an end. I'm generalizing here, and, obviously, this doesn't apply to all people, but it is an accepted approach practiced by many in these generations. Getting someone excited about working overtime for more money is not always possible. The value of time to pursue their avocation is greater than the extra money earned in their vocation. I've heard it said that previous generations lived to work, and the newer ones work to live. When assembling your staff, you need to keep in mind the true motivators that people respond to and be flexible in your approach while balancing the needs of the organization.

Fair compensation

I also understand that being cordial, interested, and even committed to your staff's personal accomplishments and professional contributions does not address the financial big picture: We are in business to make a profit. To retain the best employees, it helps to pay decent wages, but the way in which you pay those wages can affect the company's ethical culture and trust from the customer.

Let me share an example. In the HVAC industry, it's very common for technicians to get paid a percentage of the repair ticket or commissions on parts that they use in a repair. The customer must trust the technician, who shows up at their house and suggests all sorts of expensive parts and repairs; however, knowing that the technicians often receive a commission on those repairs makes that trust more difficult.

So how do we reward our staff without compromising the trust our customers have placed in us? Our technicians are not compensated through commissions. They are paid a very good hourly wage for their education and expertise and to repair the system. They are not burdened by sales quotas or commissions, and there is no incentive for upselling the customer on unnecessary parts.

Compensation and the leader's intention must align. The leader must supply the *why* behind the principles that the company follows. How those principles are implemented must align with why they are implemented.

Staff appreciation

Since two months after I assumed a leadership role, every single Friday, I put a positive note in the paycheck envelopes. In these notes, I use a quote by someone I admire or a Bible verse. Then I take the time to write something about that and how it relates to life, the company, or whatever might inspire my staff. It's worth noting that I get as many comments from spouses as from the employees that they can't wait to read them each week. This is another way to uphold morale and to minister to people in a subtle way inside the company.

Mark Twain once said, "I could live for two months on a good compliment." Sharing positive thoughts and reminders that your staff is meaningful and worthy of believing in themselves and your company exemplifies leadership that makes a difference.

When was the last time you conveyed to the people with the least seniority at your company that you are grateful to them for their contributions? How about your right-hand executive? When was the last time you asked about her family? When did you last take a stroll through your client care center to simply say thank you to the people who answer your phones?

We also show our appreciation by catching people doing the right thing and holding that up in front of people in our company. Our "Atta' Bucks" system begins when a customer writes in to share a positive experience. The customer's comments are read aloud in front of everyone at the relevant employee's departmental service meeting. The employees collect "Atta' Bucks," which they can redeem for gift cards. We also award "Safety Bucks" every month to people who remain accident free. Also, personnel can nominate other staff members for going above and beyond.

Beyond creating meaningful events that help your staff know they're appreciated and valued, there are so many little things you, as a leader, can do to lead with valiance and grace. These range from the simplest of compliments to financial incentives.

In addition to these tokens of our appreciation, I instituted something called The Joy Committee. It is designed for boosting morale with employees and making sure we are looking out for them on multiple fronts. The Joy Committee brings the lighthearted side of corporate culture to the workplace.

Find someone who exemplifies joy in your company to lead the charge and get creative with your staff.

The Joy Committee maps out fun things for our team, which can include anything from a hot dog cookout for the opening day of baseball season to any number of things we do to lighten the load.

The saying goes, "There is no such thing as a free lunch," so of course there is always a cost to the company associated with these events. But they are minor in comparison to the return on such investments. Find someone who exemplifies joy in your company to lead the charge and get creative with your staff.

At Conditioned Air, our Joy Committee supplements the other areas when applicable. Sometimes rewarding hard, purposeful work is as simple as a hot dog cookout or an ice cream day.

Take advice from your experienced employees

Let's talk about communication for a moment. The main point of communication is to express thoughts to other people so that those thoughts can be understood. It may seem easier to simply communicate a message by firing off a quick email. Nothing is a substitute for face time with your staff, particularly when your staff is on the younger side. Body language, tone, and the interaction that can occur are very valuable.

There is no substitute for youth and the spunk that they have.

Although you have to harness that, you also have to direct it. If you have young staff members who are hungry to take risks, your company will thrive from their energy. There are smaller organizations founded with very young people who have not had the benefit of trials and tribulations. If your company is in that category, then consider hiring older staff members who have wisdom to share to be that counterpoint. This creates a balanced work environment and may help avoid pitfalls.

It's important to hear the viewpoints of your staff—both those who are young in their careers and others who may have spent a lifetime in the workforce. When I inherited the task of growing Conditioned Air twenty years ago, a handful of people were still working at the company who had been there twenty years before me. What is the secret of retaining talent like that? Is there a way to hire for life?

Our oldest employee is named Shorty. He is a true professional, a service technician, and he is as happy as a lark to have been with us for more than forty-five years. In the area of human resources, I don't think leaders can overestimate the influence they can have when they create a personal relationship with their employees. For example, picking up the phone and calling your employees to congratulate them on an accomplishment, such as passing a very rigorous exam, means a lot to them, and it's the right thing to do.

I have had employees with family members in hospice, and I have stopped by to visit them. The employees appreciate that compassion—just a hug or saying you're thinking of them or praying for them.

We attract compassionate people because of the reputation we have established in the workplace. We have a lot of customer referrals, but we also have a lot of employee referrals. It is a huge help in recruiting people, and I think it is a big compliment to the management staff and what we practice. People get hired here all the time, and when I see them afterward, I always walk out from behind the desk and say hello to the new hires, no matter how busy I am.

Professional development— for management too

The tools of management and leadership are different from the tools of our field personnel. We invest in proper vehicles to run service for our clients. We invest in locations, buildings, tools, and equipment. It should be no different with our management teams, including the leaders. We must also invest in continuing education for our technical staff. This is all part of working smarter. We already work hard. The combination of the two—a well-laid-out plan and the proper knowledge to accomplish the plan—yields an efficient operation.

There is a story of a lumberjack contest that pitted a young boy against a well-experienced cutter to see who could chop the most wood in an hour. Logs were stacked up in massive piles, and the day came for the contest. The crowd was filled with great anticipation as the whistle was about to set the two opponents in motion.

The whistle blew, and with that, the mighty lumberjack struck the first blow into a log. The boy, meanwhile, stared at his ax and sat down with his back to his opponent. The boy got up in a minute and began swinging. With every hit of the blade, the wood flew. The lumberjack kept swinging and splitting logs. About ten minutes passed, and the boy sat down again. This pattern kept up for the next fifty minutes. At the end of the hour, the logs were counted.

The crowd grew quiet as the judge announced the winner: The young man had beaten the favored, experienced lumberjack. In disbelief, the lumberjack counted the logs himself and with indignation said to the boy, "Every few minutes, I'd look over to see you resting on the stump and not doing anything. Meanwhile, I kept swinging away. How is it you could beat me while wasting time?"

The boy answered, "Sir, I was not resting or wasting time. I was sharpening my ax. I just figured a sharp ax would make my work easier."

How often do we rush into our work and not take the time necessary to sharpen our ax? By that, I mean a couple of things: First, we should plan the task at hand and apply some thought as to how to get it done efficiently and done right. And, second, we should take time to gain knowledge through education and skills training so we have more tools available to us to address a situation better prepared. This is an essential part of productivity.

If you are the smartest person in the business, then you are the limiting factor for the whole organization.

If you and I are not willing to take the time to go through self-improvement, our demand on fellow teammates rings hollow. Leadership is just that—leading—not pushing. Striving to learn new techniques, theories, and practical ways to run our companies is, at the very least, selfishly in our own best interest. A lack of education for every team member should not be the limiting factor putting a ceiling on our company growth. If you are the smartest person in the business, then you are the limiting factor for the whole organization. In fact, author John Maxwell calls this the "law of the lid."[5] By continuing to make smarter people out of the ones that surround you, the company rises, and you with it.

A couple of paragraphs ago, I used the word *invest* repeatedly. I chose to repeat the word several times to stress a point: It takes time to raise the management education level enough to see a payoff from it. This is very different from a quick-fix approach or a one-time workshop. Education is continuous. It has to have a high priority set by you. It is interactive, implemented, and reviewed. The results take time to realize. Missteps must be tolerated along the way to allow for trial and error, and success. This is a difficult process for owners with a controlling nature. These are, however, necessary growing pains. As the organization's level of professionalism is increased, so is the level of expectation for and from all the team members. You can't get an A+ company with C– players, even if you are an A+ yourself. The more you invest in management and leadership skills, the higher the company flies. Instead of a downward spiral into the abyss of mediocrity, you create an upward staircase toward superiority.

The owner or president of the company can sometimes instill some practices in management meetings. But even if you participate in periodic management education classes, running back with the idea du jour and asking people to implement what you just heard is not wise. These ideas soon lose their appeal and are soon replaced by yet another idea. No focused effort or momentum is created, and consequently, nothing productive comes from this. Investing in a trusted education format that focuses on managerial growth is very valuable. Often, learning by sharing with others in the class is as meaningful and effective as the course itself. Your staff knows the value of the education, and it becomes a benefit of being on the team. It also creates camaraderie among the team and peer accountability: *If he or she can do this, so can I.*

It is said that talk is cheap. Not in this case. The goal is to turn the "talk" into the "walk." Implementation of the ideas learned is the payoff to the education scenario. The off-site program my management team is enrolled in covers the following topics: leading high-performance teams, personal development, effective leadership for executives, cutting-edge communication techniques for leaders, morale boosting and team building, performance management and appraisal, creating environments that get results, and the power of an aligned team. There are a number of ways to tap various programs that speak to the needs of leadership development. Mine happens to be through an independent business coach that coordinates the speakers and facilitates the implementation sessions. Such coaches exist in nearly all communities along with many programs hosted by community colleges, chambers of commerce, and economic development councils.

Our group meets eight times per year with other managers from many other types of businesses. Our business coach is also present. The group listens to and interacts with a speaker and then dedicates the afternoon to holding various discussions on the topic. However, one key to making this program truly successful is that one month after each topic is taught and discussed, we host an implementation session to focus on the topic and design how to effectively introduce the ideas into the managers' respective departments. This is the tactical side of business education: how to use and integrate it daily.

The topics are not HVAC specific. Rather, they deal with general management or business principles that all businesses must use. All of our leaders enjoy the classes and comparing management issues with others in the class. It is refreshing and eye opening to see that these problems and opportunities transcend different businesses and industries. Realizing you are not alone in your own world of leadership is valuable. I don't expect managers to use every idea that they hear. I expect them to filter the good ones from the bad ones and use those that make the most sense in their areas of responsibility. Remember, you can teach good business principles but you must hire good judgment and ethics.

Proper business education is the essential element to set someone up for success and, consequently, to set your company up for success as well.

As we discussed earlier, in many cases, managers rise to their level by being good in industry-specific skill sets—for instance, service managers being just that because they were good field techs. But now we have thrown them into the role as a profit manager with no real skills to understand pricing issues, finances, personnel leadership, conflict resolution, and so on. Without realizing it, we can easily set people up for failure while thinking we have just promoted them to their rightful position. Our frustration and disbelief comes when they underwhelm us in their performance, but we remember how good they were one step prior. Proper business education is the essential element to set someone up for success and, consequently, to set your company up for success as well.

It costs time and money to put an education program in place for management. It must be made a high priority by the head of the company for results to be seen. But the time and money it costs not to have an educated team is much greater. To rise above much of the competition, make a commitment to business education. The hard work will always be there but it will seem easier with improved efficiency. It's kind of like having a sharp ax in a woodcutting contest.

Leadership Heartbeats

- Keep in mind the true motivators that team members respond to.
- Compensation and the leader's intention must align.
- Exemplify leadership that makes a difference by sharing positive thoughts and reminders that your team members are meaningful and worthy of believing in themselves and your company.
- Listen to the viewpoints of your experienced team members and your not-so-experienced team members.
- Invest in continuing education and self-improvement for all team members—including leaders—to rise above much of your competition.
- Make serving and supporting your staff a priority.

CHAPTER 13

AVOIDING BURNOUT

"By the seventh day God had finished the
work he had been doing; so on the seventh day
he rested from all his work."

—GENESIS 2:2

There is an old adage that says, "It's better to burn out than fade away." But in reality—for company executives and support staff—neither are healthful ways to operate. Exercise caution when you're not at your best. Because every day, you want your customers, and your employees for that matter, to vote for the company, and you, the leader, will dictate the atmosphere at your office.

Shorter hours, more money, happier employees, less stress, clear future, longer vacations, all is great with the world. Is this your reality? I hope so, but I would guess that this may be reality for only a very small percentage of us. Cutting across many industry and business lines, I hear and see the reality of having to do more with less, lower margins, tight cash, high stress levels in staff, more demanding clients, shorter tempers, an uncertain economic future, and longer hours that still never seem to be enough. Not only can you, the leader of a company, experience burnout, but the entire organization can suffer from it as well.

What is *burnout*? Simply stated, it is a feeling of being overwhelmed and not able to make a significant difference in the outcome of events, over a sustained period of time. This is a feeling that builds. It is also influenced by personal demands, civic demands, and pressure on yourself to maintain a certain lifestyle or community persona. Allowed to manifest fully, a general apathy creeps into the subconscious and then the conscious thought process. Symptoms and physical actions then follow. If the leader exhibits these traits, the employees and clients will follow suit, which can damage the organization's viability.

Let me say right here that burnout is vastly different from temporary frustrations in the everyday games of business and life. We all experience periods of frustration when a situation does not resolve itself quickly or is out of our control for a while. These are normal occurrences, and we rise to the challenge and fight the good fight. If we find that we have lost the desire to jump into the fight and the feeling of not caring or an almost give-up-or-give-in attitude exists, then we need a deeper examination of where we really are in life. This "not caring" feeling can be a true sign of burnout.

Workplace balance

Avoiding burnout scenarios in the staff's experience at work is one of the main responsibilities of the leader of the company. Remember, leaders wear many hats and are always on stage, so everyone is looking at you for the tone and direction and general mood of the company. To reinforce the positive morale of each employee and of your entire work group,

- recognize people for a job well done,
- make sure they feel like an integral part of the whole team and that they have a purpose for being there, and
- provide growth opportunities through education and advancement.

We instituted our Joy Committee, which comes up with simple, fun ideas to break the tension of work once in a while. It could be wearing your favorite team jersey to work, free pizza for lunch, a putting contest, or the like, but people enjoy the laughs and the break in routine. Seeing the leader laugh at himself or herself is a great stress reliever for the team.

Leaders wear many hats and are always on stage, so everyone is looking at you for the tone and direction and general mood of the company.

We all experience fatigue from economic malaise, from the political tug-of-war and polarization of ideologies, and from news on battlefronts many miles from home. People, both inside and outside the company, feel worn out. In recent years, many companies have had to lay off staff and cut hours. These actions, while necessary, transfer more work to fewer people, again causing people to feel like there's too much work and not enough time. Paying attention to balance in the workplace is very important. If people are not allowed to find fun or rewards in what they do, burnout is not far behind. This goes for the leadership as well.

Since the late 1990s, both the rate of change of technology and the expectations placed on people in the workplace have accelerated at a staggering pace. Who can't relate to the idea of learning a software program and, just when you get comfortable, a new and improved version comes out, and the learning curve starts all over again? This causes anxiety for people, because most often our natural tendency is to resist change.

I think it is very important for people to understand not only how to do specific jobs inside the business but also what they are truly doing for the greater purpose of the organization and its customers. We all need to know this, including the leader. How we do something and what we do are very different. The *how* might be through the use of a computer, meters, telephone, or pager. The *what* is to provide comfort and safety for people who need help with cooling, heating, and indoor air quality, in my case. The *what* speaks to our purpose and the greater good of why we find satisfaction in going to work. As a leader, you should embrace this concept and communicate it to your employees. We may also avoid our own feeling of burnout when we repeat our purpose to ourselves.

Set boundaries and take time to recharge

Many years ago, I told my employer that I was going to take a "working vacation," and he said: "Okay, but it won't be good work, and it won't be a good vacation." I was too young to truly understand his advice, but I realized after I returned to work that I hadn't done the work I had taken, and I really hadn't relaxed like I thought I would. In fact, I remember feeling somewhat unproductive and certainly not mentally rested. I tell this story because it is truer today for more people and on a daily basis. The reason: connectivity through technology.

When you, as the leader, allow activity to be mistaken for productivity, you've created the perfect environment for employee burnout.

Wow, are we connected! Leaders and staff members alike can be connected to the office 24–7–365. The lines of work time and personal time have become blurred—and completely erased for some. Being "on" for clients, staff, and colleagues means being "off" for others, possibly family members or yourself.

When you, as the leader, allow activity to be mistaken

for productivity, you've created the perfect environment for employee burnout. So it stands to reason that if the power of learning is the best weapon against mediocrity, a well-managed workload is the antidote to burnout.

Knowing work patterns and setting limits on them for both you and your employees is crucial in reducing the chances of burnout. This is easier said than done, especially today, with more demanding customers and shorter reaction times. The need to set boundaries is greater than ever before. If we don't take time to recharge our batteries, we have no other outcome except frustration and burnout. I know that's a strong statement, but balance in life is so important to our overall well-being that it can hardly be overstated.

Signs of burnout

People who are high achievers, who set high standards and high goals, are more prone to suffer burnout as their career develops than hardworking realists. Life, and especially business life, isn't perfect. When the reality of the situation continues to fall short of perfection and does not measure up to people's ideals, they may experience burnout. This is not to say that lofty goals and the desire for exceptional outcomes are bad things. But we need to be mindful that the failure to meet unrealistic goals will defeat the most optimistic person over time. Paying attention to your own feelings is very important. But watching out for signs that an employee is beginning to suffer from burnout is critical for the success of the organization.

People who suffer from burnout often feel fatigued, emotionally sapped, and tired just handling the day-to-day grind. Tempers can get a little short, or a reaction may seem like an overreaction to a small incident. You might see people who are much less productive than they were before or who exhibit less attention or more apathy. Certainly, over the past few years many people have been put in the position of having to lay people off, close locations, or utilize other downsizing efforts. Making significant cutbacks in all areas is very stressful. Managers and leaders may often appear melancholy or even depressed because they are in this cycle. Burnout has a sense of hopelessness associated with it. People may refer to this state as being *stressed out*. In any event, the desire to go climb another mountain, whatever that is in life at the time, is simply not there.

Some people cope by masking the discomfort of stress and burnout with alcohol or drugs or other diversionary addictions. Obviously, this behavior only leads to destruction, not only of this person but also to all others associated with them. If this is you or someone you know, I strongly recommend arranging for professional intervention.

Work–life balance

So, what can we do to avoid a downward spiral to the land of burnout? I believe the first thing to do is acknowledge that it can happen to any of us. If we pretend it doesn't exist, it can sneak up and catch you by surprise. Put it out on the table, and say that you want to make sure it doesn't happen by paying attention to the signs mentioned here. Use the potential of a burnout situation to reevaluate your priorities in life, and seek the balance that is needed. Remember the example of the three-legged stool: When one leg gets disproportionately long or short, the stool collapses. Balance among work, personal time, family, spirituality, and community involvement can be difficult and must be approached proactively. Certainly, there are times in our lives when we need to focus more attention on one area because of demanding circumstances that require our time and energy. But when that short-term focus becomes a long-term, seemingly endless commitment, that's when trouble can begin.

I once wrote an article about my use of a business coach. Not to revisit the entire concept here, but one of the goals in these coaching sessions is the discussion of checks and balances in my work and personal life to help keep me centered. My monthly meetings with other CEOs also help me gain perspective in the broader picture of business and personal issues.

Burnout will occur. It can happen to you, me, or someone we know. If we acknowledge this fact and take proactive steps to keep our lives in balance and our priorities in perspective, we can work to avoid these repetitive cycles that so many people experience. I believe in taking big challenges and breaking them into smaller, more manageable tasks. Feeling overwhelmed is a very uncomfortable feeling. We've all heard the expression "How do you eat an elephant? One bite at a time." Be up-front and assertive in managing burnout and addressing the steps to avoid it. Don't let burnout be an elephant you have to eat.

I'd rather choose the path of less corporate fame and fortune for the sake of balance, for time with my family and for myself. And I want the same for my employees—for them to have a life away from the office. I want my staff to be proud of the work they do and to know their families too. A happier employee is a more productive employee.

Many times, I have sent people home to go work on a personal problem that is overwhelming them. This should also apply to you. If my heart wants to be somewhere else, then I'm really not that useful at work.

Here's an example. We're called to make choices in life—I know I should be at my child's play, but I have a business dinner I'd really like to go to. As a leader, I have to prioritize which areas to invest in and at which times. Going to my business dinner, sitting there regretful or distracted, isn't productive for the business and certainly isn't beneficial to my family.

I can recall two separate opportunities, years apart, when I was invited to attend exclusive golf trips with the men in my extended family. One conflicted with my son's confirmation, and one was during my daughter's confirmation. I knew where I had to be. I knew that if I was away playing golf, I would regret not being with my children on their journey.

Guess what—I got to go play later when there wasn't a

conflict. I knew I would have been miserable if I hadn't made those choices. It is important for people to be where their heart is—if at all possible, their body needs to be in that same spot. They need to be aligned. It is not worth the internal anguish that you know will strike if you don't make the right choices. And every time I have followed that advice, I've been blessed by my choices. Sure, some people thought I was crazy, but it was the right thing to do.

Everyone has had tough times in life. I certainly have, especially when faced with a situation that needed my devotion and that I couldn't block out of my mind. I needed to handle those issues first and get to a pausing point before I could focus on other things. If something is interfering with your ability at work, take the time to go fix it.

Leadership Heartbeats

- Reinforce the positive morale of each team member and of your entire work group.
- Strive to maintain balance in the workplace—balance between work and fun/rewards.
- Set boundaries and take time to recharge.
- Be aware of signs of burnout in yourself and others.
- Take proactive steps to keep balance among work, personal time, family, spirituality, and community involvement for yourself and your team members.

CHAPTER 14

THE BUSINESS OF DISCIPLINE

*"Discipline is the soul of an army. It makes
small numbers formidable; procures success
to the weak, and esteem to all."*

—GEORGE WASHINGTON

In developing a good staff, you have to weed the garden. There is no getting around that. And this is where you can't be arbitrary or capricious. It's easier sometimes to make exceptions, especially in the heat of business, because people are imperfect and things are imperfect. But you have to work through those imperfections the best you can, and that includes disciplinary action. It may seem easier to be the nice guy by not holding someone accountable, but that is a slippery slope. You must follow through. Be consistent and fair in administering discipline.

Hold all your employees—and yourself—accountable, impart the rules. Because when you let exceptions become the rule, your rules become meaningless.

When you let exceptions become the rule,
your rules become meaningless.

This holds true when it is a personnel problem and when you're dealing with consumers in the marketplace. Be judicious, fair, and equitable, but all those terms are relative to a solid right and wrong.

Only buck the system when it matters

In business, you'll often encounter staff members who haven't had a perfect experience with their previous supervisors. They might have been asked at one point or another to do something totally against their principles. They should always have the right to speak out about that.

However, you and your staff members need to know that bucking the system when it isn't based on a principle is not good for the company. In a classroom setting, when a teacher tells you to turn in homework in black ink, it's smart to do so. Using a different color is not a principled action; it's a preference. In a classroom setting, someone is always prepared to buck the system just because, to resist authority without a reason. Don't let that be you. And don't put up with it from your employees.

When, however, you have people who want to buck the system on your team, my experience has been that there is very little you can do to change their behavior. It is best to let them upset someone else's apple cart. It's tempting to keep a person working on a project even though they are troublesome. And, at times, it is worth the effort to coach, to help a worthy individual turn things around, and to keep them as a valued part of the team.

CEOs sometimes have a hard time disciplining their staff because doing so will mean more work for the leader, so they make exceptions. But in the long run, this practice hurts the organization and your ability to lead. This is where leaders have to be strong and recognize that the short-term pain associated with letting someone go and taking on more work themselves in the interim is really an investment in the future. It may not be convenient and creates momentary interruptions to your schedule, but the message it sends to the rest of the staff—that you value them more than your own comfort—is well worth it.

Bad employees are contagious. There is a difference between someone misplaced in the company and someone who doesn't have the skill set or properly fit the cultural attitude of the company. If the employee is misplaced, it's a disservice to that person and your company, and it's up to the leader to fix that. If they are in the wrong position but a good person, move them to where they can be successful. They'll be happier, and their contribution factor will skyrocket.

There is a famous scene in *Star Trek II: The Wrath of Khan* where Spock dies, and just before that he says, "The needs of the many outweigh the needs of the few, or the one." From a leadership point of view, that is a kernel of truth. We wonder whether we should keep people who are not living up to their responsibilities, because they need a job and a paycheck. Keeping a bad employee and accepting poor behavior and performance could jeopardize the lives and incomes of all the other people who are contributing to a balanced work environment.

To make the decision about your mediocre employee, outline where that person needs to be, what needs to happen within a specific time frame, and the consequences to the employee of not reaching those expectations. Hold weekly meetings with that employee. Tell them that employment is something they need to work for and that it requires a commitment. If they don't want to do that, it's okay. They should know that if they do not meet the expectations by the end of the specified time period, they will no longer be a part of the company. Whatever your rules are for your organization, you have to be firm.

We have had success stories with people who have turned it around, but we also employ a thirty- to ninety-day corrective action plan. I fully believe in being fair when letting people go, and it should never be a surprise to that person. In this plan, we reemphasize in great detail the ways in which we want the employee to behave. There are no gray areas. During the probation period, we touch base weekly. When you incorporate such an action, you will know quickly whether employees will work out or whether they need to go. They end up either saving their job or firing themselves.

Leadership Heartbeats

- Be consistent and fair in administering discipline.
- Make no exceptions.
- "The needs of the many outweigh the needs of the few, or the one."
- Whatever your rules are for your organization, you have to be firm.

CHAPTER 15

DOING THE
RIGHT THING

"The time is always right to do what is right."

—MARTIN LUTHER KING JR.

In a capitalist society, one truth is that you are in business to produce a profit. The flip side is that if you do not produce a profit, you do not get to stay in the game. It's up to you to figure out how you're going to make a profit, and in the United States, you have many avenues to do so. I choose to conduct business in a manner that works with my values. I also believe that unethical or selfish CEOs do not last long, and those attributes are not the pathway to making a profit. That said, I do not feel guilty about ethically earning a profit. Many executives, particularly of the younger generation, are also socially conscious. They might feel concern that they are profiting while so many businesses or individuals go without.

But profitable businesses are some of the greatest social bene-factors on earth. We provide incomes to families, housing, food on tables, and education. Having a profitable business is one of the greatest social services you can provide.

Ethics

I never took a class on business ethics in college; it wasn't even offered then. I think I know when wrong is wrong. That's why I don't separate personal behavior from business ethics. At Con-ditioned Air, we try to empower our team members to provide solutions in an ethical way. That means only selling solutions that the customer needs or wants, not padding the bill with unneeded parts and pieces.

Beyond the biblical principles by which I try to govern my company and life, there are just basic right or wrong ways to do things that directly affect your bottom line. It may seem sim-ple to take the easiest route, such as to offer commissions that tempt your staff to stray from ethical behavior with customers. But in the long run, there are far better ways to manage that allow everyone to benefit and to sleep at night while doing so.

Making the right choices in an ethical
manner is a long-term investment.

Business ethics isn't new, but leaders recently seem to want right and wrong to be relative, the gray area between them to be expansive. But, actually, you must be anchored in an absolute, or everything is gray area, the right and the wrong always relative and flowing. When you, as a leader, allow things to become gray, the need for hard and fast rules is more important than ever. There is a cost involved in making a tough decision that follows the path of the right, but it is a short-term cost for long-term gains. Making the right choices in an ethical manner is a long-term investment.

Too many veteran executives have lost sight of business ethics in America. Too few next-generation business leaders learn what they need to know about business ethics in school. But ethics in business remains one of the most important tools an executive has to blaze a fortuitous trail. When it can seem so easy to go the carefree route, why would you base your business on ethics, doing things the right way? Simply put, it will benefit you and your company in the long run.

Every day is an election

Our team does a great job, but that does not come without a lot of focused effort. Our true employers are outside this building. Our customers vote with their dollars, which means we must have a corporate culture that supports that.

All of our employees understand that the customers are really their employers. Therefore, the number one mission in our office is to serve our employees out in the field, while they are serving our customers in a one-to-one, face-to-face setting.

My staff needs our support to do that, and as a leader, part of my job is to see that they have it in all areas.

Here is a simple equation to understanding where you register on the success scale. It's easy to know if you're winning or losing in business because customers vote with their dollars. That's how customers cast their ballots. They vote for you—or for someone else. Every day is an election.

Customers vote with their dollars.

There are two lessons here—one is that you need to be at your best for new customers. But the other lesson is that you want customers to repeatedly spend money with you. That's your real affirmation that you're doing things correctly. Thanks to customers who are willing to come back and spend more money with your company, you can survive for some time. Churning new customers, or getting someone to try out your business, is expensive. And worse, if you stop providing a service or product that current customers perceive as a good value, they'll stop voting for you. Their perception is reality to them.

Community outreach

Business advisor Richard F. Schubert said, "Giving of ourselves is the way we change the world at the end of our fingertips."

Companies that invest in the community do change the world. But incorporating charitable efforts in modern marketing methods can make a company appear insincere. Be guarded about how donating time or money or product to charity might look to your customers. If your motivation is simply to gain publicity, your plan can backfire. You can be seen as trite or insincere; tooting your own horn and waving a big banner won't draw people to your company.

If you decide to do something for the good of the community, do so from an altruistic place. Here is a small example of how this practice actually does help the community, which will organically help your business. When I was in the ice cream business, we adopted an elementary school and gave each student a free cone when they completed a reading program. The kids loved to come in with their certificate to get a treat. This wasn't for publicity; we did it because we wanted to do it. It was just part of being in the community.

We also did other community events simply because they were fun and used ice cream to raise morale in a difficult time. We gave away a totally free cone once a year on tax day. One year, we gave away 5,000 cones in that single day. Yes, this generated publicity, but that wasn't why we did it.

A news van happened to be in the area and the reporter heard about the ice cream giveaway. With nothing to do between stories, he called and said, "We're going to stop and do a remote there at your store." You can do something that is outside the norm, especially if you have a product you can sample; nothing makes a bigger impression than your product. Do you want to look at a picture of ice cream in the paper or do you want to taste it?

As we all know, communities everywhere have projects and needs that require support beyond what tax dollars can fund. Individuals give in many ways and for many reasons. But businesses have the opportunity to make contributions in time, resources, people, and money to support organizations that add value and life to the community in which the business is located. Of course, your contributions are not limited geographically; you can support worldwide efforts as well. But there are many smaller, lesser-known organizations trying to make a positive difference right in our backyards. These are the groups that need our support. A better local community is the "world at the end of our fingertips," where we can make a difference for our neighbors, standing side by side.

I was in a discussion recently—more along the lines of a debate—where the idea of giving back was presented more as a quid pro quo. One person's contention was that she would only donate resources to organizations that could demonstrate that their supporters or members had done or were doing business with her company. Her company only donated with the full expectation that there was something in it for them. I must say that I am 180 degrees removed from this philosophy when it comes to charitable work. Giving should be from the heart.

have found that this form of support does breed loyalty; the parents of the team members go out of their way to support or recommend us for their air conditioning needs. Again, you will be disappointed if you expect people to run to you just because you bought an ad from a sports booster, but experience has shown this to be a partnership form of support and advertising or sponsorship that leads to brand loyalty. Many groups need sponsors, including charities running golf tournaments, churches, chambers of commerce, and the like. We budget advertising dollars for these as opposed to donation dollars because we get recognition in return.

We also invite our employees to participate in organizations and to bring opportunities for financial support to our attention. Again, while we may not be able to say yes to everything, we try very hard to support something that is important to one of our employees. Demonstrating that we value what they value goes a long way in showing that we support them and reinforces their feeling of belonging. Of course, if you can't philosophically support their cause, you must stay true to your beliefs.

The mainstay of being a good corporate citizen is remaining profitable. Then, and only then, can you afford to employ people, provide opportunities for them, and have money to donate to community organizations. The purpose of business is to make money. What you do with that money is then your decision, and without money, there is no decision to make. The more efficient and profitable you are, the more choices you have regarding your distribution of those profits. In many cases, leading by example can influence what people do to support the community, and you can sway other businesses to support valuable organizations for a better society.

The mainstay of being a good corporate
citizen is remaining profitable.

We, as business owners, have the opportunity to positively affect our world every day just by doing the right things for our customers, our employees, our vendors, and our community. Treating people with honesty and integrity in all that we do is the right thing to do, and we should be expected to do it. This also sets a great example for the people around us, because our senses are attacked by so many messages that would have us believe that looking out for ourselves, at any price, is all that matters. Being a consistent, positive role model carries a lot of weight.

I believe that business owners have the obligation to invest in people and organizations in our communities. I also believe that these need to be looked at as gifts, with no strings attached, no expectation of increased business. If your heart is not in the organizations you wish to support, it will certainly be evident. Passion for your cause is contagious. It's this excitement that creates positive change at a local level. And this local change results in ever-increasing rings of change radiating out across this great country. And it all starts at the end of our fingertips.

Leadership Heartbeats

- Empower your team members to provide solutions in an ethical way.
- Every day is an election because customers vote with their dollars.
- Practice charitable efforts from an altruistic place.
- Remember Matthew 6:3: "But when you give to the needy, do not let your left hand know what your right hand is doing."

CHAPTER 16

BIBLICAL PRINCIPLES

"Blessed are those who hunger and thirst for
righteousness, for they will be filled."

—MATTHEW 5:6

No matter your religion or lack thereof, there's no denying the power of the Bible in growing America's top companies. And ministers and other faith leaders are increasingly obtaining degrees in business to better run their organizations.

The connection between religion and business has never been stronger and is helping both sides of the fence modernize and streamline via biblical management philosophy. Here are just a few successful businesses running on biblical principles:

- Tyson Foods has a team of chaplains available to minister to its employees.[6]

- Hobby Lobby includes a biblical statement in its mission text—"We are committed to . . . Honoring the Lord in all we do by operating the company in a manner consistent with Biblical principles."[7]

- Mary Kay Ash founded Mary Kay cosmetics on the belief that "God has blessed us because our motivation is right. He knows I want women to be the beautiful creatures He created."[8]

- Truett Cathy proved that Chick-fil-A could be very successful and still hold to being closed on Sundays to give his employees a chance to be with family and go to church together. In a 2004 interview, Truett stated, "I see no conflict whatsoever between Christianity and good business practices . . . People say you can't mix business with religion. I say there's no other way."[9]

- The popular fast food chain In-N-Out Burger is known for printing Bible verses on the inside of its drink cups. President and CEO Richard Snyder asked for biblical verses to be printed on the wrappers and cups in 1987, and the company continues the tradition even though Snyder died in 1993. A company spokesman recalled Snyder saying, "It's just something I want to do."[10]

- Timberland CEO Jeff Swartz attributes his commitment to promoting corporate social responsibility to a Hebrew phrase meaning "treat a stranger with dignity." Swartz severed ties with a factory where human rights violations were occurring even though it resulted in the company taking a hit.[11]

- For thirty years, up until February 1, 2012, Alaska Airlines used to serve passengers meal trays that came with an inspirational passage from the Old Testament printed on a note card.[12] The quotes were shared as a gesture of thanks.

- Marriott Hotel founder John Willard Marriott was a devout Mormon. The hotel chain is now known for putting the Book of Mormon alongside the Bible in hotel rooms.[13]

- The founder and CEO of JetBlue Airlines, David Neeleman, once traveled to Brazil as a Mormon missionary. His missionary experience is reflected in JetBlue's prized customer service. "My missionary experience obliterated class distinction for me," he said. "I learned to treat everyone the same."[14] Neeleman has since gone on to establish Azul Airlines in Brazil. *Azul* means "blue" in Portuguese. He founded it to provide low-cost, fast transportation to people in underserved markets and small cities in Brazil.

- According to Interstate Batteries' website, their purpose is "To glorify God and enrich lives as we deliver the most trustworthy source of power to the world."[15]

- ServiceMaster owns household names like Merry Maids and Terminix. The company's foundational commitment is to "honor God in all we do."[16]

- Tom's of Maine, the natural products retailer, is purposely treated like a ministry by CEO Tom Chappell. Chappell's mission statement even says, "To help create a better world by exchanging our faith, experience, and hope."[17]

The list of millionaires and billionaires who incorporate faith-based management in their business practices is staggering. My faith plays a major role in my personal and business life. It has shaped the way I've operated my businesses throughout the years and helped hold my team and me accountable. I've applied many biblical principles to my business model with tremendous success, and even if this isn't your path, I hope you'll keep reading to learn how faith has played a major role in my success and the success of my businesses.

Trust your GUT

When you're investing your heartbeats, nothing is more important than trusting your gut. *Gut* means different things to different people—your instinct, your core. For me, it's an acronym: GUT, standing for *God uttered thoughts*. It's my inner self—that still, small voice of God talking to me that gives me a feeling for what is or is not quite right.

Any time I have gone against my GUT, things didn't work out. This has been especially true when I've tried to force a deal. In the past, when it hasn't seemed like something is meant to be or I would have had to force something to fit a particular situation, my instincts were correct—and the deal fell through.

It took a few years of experience and a few conversations with the Lord to get me to trust my GUT. I really rely on the fact that I pray for wisdom and judgment—for the safety of the people who work with me and for the way we do things as a company. For me, that is part of honoring the way I think we're supposed to live.

You, as the leader of your organization, must become seasoned at understanding when you can make a decision. The best part of that equation is—you guessed it—your very own GUT. Ask yourself, "Does this feel right?" Listen, be open to the Lord, and trust His direction. It will always serve you well.

I'm a fan of poetry—writing it and reading it. When writing poetry, sometimes, all of a sudden, I have to get to a keyboard and let go; I just have to get those thoughts down. When your GUT speaks, never fail to jot down what you're thinking. Those thoughts could one day become meaningful as you develop an inner sense of what's right and wrong in your decision-making processes.

Nowhere is listening to your GUT more important than when you must lead a staff member or even your entire company through a time of great change. That could be a massive economic downturn or the death of a longtime colleague. It could be the promotion of a devoted mentee, a major change in IT that affects everyone, or even venturing into new markets or products.

I have often found that temptation comes disguised in the form of opportunities. Use care and weigh all the unintended consequences when analyzing these. Then give them a GUT check against your right–wrong and good–bad filter. Just as we are told to be discerning when dealing with people, so should we be when we have business decisions to make. Proverbs 16:21 is a great reminder of this precept: "The wise in heart are called discerning, and gracious words promote instruction."

You must ensure that your employees are not just looking at the newest change and thinking, *Oh my goodness, this is just more work for me—all this brainstorming has all of a sudden just landed on my plate.* You need to lead them through it. Follow your GUT, and stick to your principles.

Biblical principles become core values

Conditioned Air's core values are very similar to the biblical principles that have helped people live better but that are also good business. Here are the core values we abide by at Conditioned Air, through which we reach and teach:

- integrity,
- respect,
- safety,
- purposeful effort, and
- exceeding expectations.

Integrity

"The wise in heart accepts commands, but a chattering fool comes to ruin. Whoever walks in integrity walks securely, but whoever takes crooked paths will be found out. Whoever winks maliciously causes grief and a chattering fool comes to ruin."

PROVERBS 10:8–10

Integrity, for us, is making sure our words and deeds are truthful, that we fulfill the trust that we are given by both customers and employees to be honest and factual. By not having incentives built into procedures that would cause people to stray from their integrity, we help minimize the chance for people to deviate from our values. I think we can all point to people we have known or read about that fit the model of "crooked path" people. They do fall and are exposed in the end.

Respect

"Hope deferred makes the heart sick, but a longing fulfilled is a tree of life. Whoever scorns instruction will pay for it, but whoever respects a command is rewarded. The teaching of the wise is a fountain of life turning a person from the snares of death."

PROVERBS 13:12–14

Respect has many facets. Obviously, showing respect in how we treat all people is important, especially if we wish to keep employees and clients. But we must look to a broader interpretation with this concept. The verse speaks to our ability to always be in a learning mode and to respect the wisdom we can glean from others. Furthermore, the lack of respect for instruction will cause us to fail. We take this even further when we extend this to show respect for people's property, their home or office. Taking care not to damage the customer's surroundings and to clean up after ourselves is important in showing respect for the whole person. Similarly, paying our vendors in a timely manner shows that we respect them and their efforts to help us be successful.

Safety

"For the waywardness of the simple will kill them, and the complacency of fools will destroy them, but whoever listens to me will live in safety and be at ease, without fear of harm."

PROVERBS 1:32–33

Safety is huge with us. First and foremost, I want our people to go home at the end of the day to their families and be able to hug them. I never want to have to deliver terrible news to any member of our extended family. We constantly talk about safe behavior in all we do. Protecting our employees' vision with safety glasses, proper ladder techniques, hazardous material handling, electrical lockouts—we want people to act safely in all they do on the job.

Our largest exposure is in the number of miles we travel while driving. With more than two hundred vehicles on the road, we must be vigilant to drive safely and carefully. There are practical sides to all the safety training and direct cost implications for the lack of safety. It's expensive to be careless: increased workers' compensation costs, lawsuits for traffic accidents, property damage, and a reputation for being sloppy. As the proverb says, we cannot be complacent about safety but must be intentional and proactive.

Purposeful effort

*"Sluggards do not plow in season so at harvest time they look
but find nothing. The purposes of a person's heart are
deep waters, but one who has insight draws them out."*

PROVERBS 20:4–5

We use this to remind ourselves that activity does not equal productivity. We owe it to people to be productive while working for them. In turn, we must be alert to opportunities and challenges that present themselves to us. If they pass our test, we should pursue them with purpose and intention.

Exceeding expectations

"If anyone forces you to go one mile, go with them two miles."

MATTHEW 5:41

This goes back to my belief that we should strive to be more than a *C* player or mediocre. Go above and beyond, show people that extra effort for a better outcome, and give them a little more value for their trust in us. I have found that a little extra goes a long way toward building loyalty in people. This principle is true with customers and employees alike. Our goal is to have it be a habit that all our people execute. This is not easy and takes a continuous effort.

Strive to be more than a C *player.*

Just because we have our core values does not mean we hit the mark each and every time. We are fallible; we are talking about imperfect humans, myself included. And the thought of only stating our values once or just having them posted around the office and thinking that's enough is sorely wrong. They must be repeated all the time in meetings to keep them front and center in everyone's mind, and they should be used to weigh decisions the company needs to make to see whether those decisions are in keeping with our core values. We constantly work at applying them to our daily work practices.

Looking collectively at all these core values, the roots lie in the Ten Commandments and culminate in what's known as the Golden Rule:

> *"So whatever you wish that others would do to you,*
> *do also to them, for this is the Law and the Prophets."*
>
> MATTHEW 7:12

I wrote a devotional called "The Microwaving of Society" for my church when I lived in Atlanta. It had to do with the impatience of people in the ever-speeding and ever-changing world. One of the things I touched on was that people don't mind change as much as they mind the *rate of change.* Having a set of principles to live by, that doesn't change with the rest of the world, gives you a structure, a path to follow through the world, and it can ease your anxiety about change. Can you imagine what would happen if nautical signal buoys were allowed to just drift with the tides? They wouldn't be any good to the ships they were intended to guide. Even though we have to do something new and challenging— new software, changing regulations, new procedures—often to stay competitive, the *why* we do it can remain stable. The Bible talks about walking the narrow path and how we're all tasked with finding out the Lord's will for each of us. He affirms this and then speaks to the opposite as a warning:

> *"Enter by the narrow gate. For the gate is wide and the way is*
> *easy that leads to destruction, and those who enter by it are many."*
>
> MATTHEW 7:13

We can be different from the many when we try to walk the narrow path, although it may seem more difficult at times. This is where I lean on Paul's words on persistence:

"Brothers, I do not consider that I have made it my own.
But one thing I do: forgetting what lies behind and straining
forward to what lies ahead, I press on toward the goal for
the prize of the upward call of God in Christ Jesus."

PHILIPPIANS 3:13-14

Interestingly, one of my favorite adages is frequently attributed to the Bible but, in actuality, does not have its origin there. However it still has merit in the overall philosophy of my leadership style: "This, too, shall pass." It is often associated with tough times and is a sign of hope for things to get better, with the realization that the tough times will improve with effort and the passing of time. But I also like it for its humbling reminder. When things are as good as they get, this, too, shall pass. We need to be reminded, from time to time, that rainy days will come back into our lives, sometimes with little or no notice. Therefore, enjoy the great times, be thankful for them, and rejoice in the fact that the hard times will not last.

This, too, shall pass.

There are many ways to lead. I choose the model that incorporates biblical faith, hope, and love to help guide my decisions. Grasp the humble servant approach and hospitality mentality in a sincere and genuine way. If you are struggling with your leadership style or just starting to define and develop it, I invite you to try this model. I am so thankful for the people the Lord placed in my life and who have crossed my path at just the right times to help me along the way. I'm thankful for His forgiveness when I fall short. I am most grateful for the redemptive power of Jesus Christ as my savior and friend. The Lord has provided a way to have eternal life that can't be bought or earned, no matter how hard we try to follow His commandments. We are saved by God's grace when we accept Jesus Christ as God's only son, sent to earth to accept the sins of the world (mine and yours) and to die on the cross for us.

But that can't be the end of the story, because he was resurrected on the third day and rose to be with the Father, God. He wants us there, too. Jesus walked this earth with open arms, inviting people to follow him and become his disciples. He died with open arms, there on the cross for all of humanity—everybody. This is God's gift to us, showing His love. He invites us still today to accept this gift in our hearts.

We have limited heartbeats on this earth. We have unlimited ones in heaven. The wisest investment we can make is in receiving the gift of eternal life through Jesus Christ. Your circumstances may not change immediately, but your outlook on them will as your path is revealed. The return on your investment is priceless and forever.

If you already believe this, I encourage you to keep the faith that it is the right way to approach business and life. If not, please ponder these things and pray for guidance; the invitation is there, as long as you have the heartbeats to invest.

May God bless your heartbeats on this earth, the things you can accomplish, your service to others, and the leadership influence you have on all God's children.

Leadership Heartbeats

- Trust your GUT.
- Identify core values.
- Communicate core values to all team members and repeat regularly.

RECOMMENDED READING

D. Michael Abrashoff, *It's Your Ship: Management Techniques from the Best Damn Ship in the Navy* (Grand Central Publishing, 2012).

Joseph L. Badaracco Jr., *Leading Quietly: An Unorthodox Guide to Doing the Right Thing* (Harvard Business School Press, 2002).

Marc Benioff and Karen Southwick, *Compassionate Capitalism: How Corporations Can Make Doing Good an Integral Part of Doing Well* (Career Press, 2004).

Ken Blanchard, *Leading at a Higher Level: Blanchard on Leadership and Creating High Performing Organizations* (Pearson Education, 2010).

Ori Brafman and Rod A. Beckstrom, *The Starfish and the Spider: The Unstoppable Power of Leaderless Organizations* (Penguin, 2006).

Jake Breeden, *Tipping Sacred Cows: Kick the Bad Work Habits that Masquerade as Virtues* (Wiley, 2013).

Ram Charan, *Leadership in the Era of Economic Uncertainty: Managing in a Downturn* (McGraw-Hill, 2009).

Jim Collins, *Good to Great: Why Some Companies Make the Leap . . . And Others Don't* (HarperCollins, 2001).

Michael E. Gerber, *The E-Myth Revisited: Why Most Small Businesses Don't Work and What to Do About It* (HarperCollins, 1995).

Malcolm Gladwell, *Blink: The Power of Thinking without Thinking* (Little, Brown, 2005).

Jon Huntsman, *Winners Never Cheat: Even in Difficult Times* (Pearson Education, 2011).

Spencer Johnson, *Who Moved My Cheese? An Amazing Way to Deal with Change in Your Work and in Your Life* (Putnam, 1998).

John P. Kotter, *A Sense of Urgency* (Harvard Business Press, 2008).

John Kotter and Holger Rathgeber, *Our Iceberg Is Melting: Changing and Succeeding under Any Conditions* (St. Martin's Press, 2005).

Joel Kurtzman, *Common Purpose: How Great Leaders Get Organizations to Achieve the Extraordinary* (Wiley, 2010).

Patrick Lencioni, *The Advantage: Why Organizational Health Trumps Everything Else in Business* (Jossey-Bass, 2012).

Steve Marr, *Proverbs for Business: Daily Wisdom for the Workplace* (Revell, 2001).

John C. Maxwell, *Leadership Gold: Lessons I've Learned from a Lifetime of Leading* (Thomas Nelson, 2008).

John C. Maxwell, *The 21 Indispensable Qualities of a Leader: Becoming the Person Others Will Want to Follow* (Thomas Nelson, 1999).

John C. Maxwell, *The 360 Degree Leader: Developing Your Influence from Anywhere in the Organization* (Thomas Nelson, 2005).

Joseph Michelli, *The Zappos Experience: 5 Principles to Inspire, Engage, and WOW* (McGraw-Hill, 2012).

Jay Rifenbary, *No Excuse! Incorporating Core Values, Accountability, and Balance into Your Life and Career* (Possibility Press, 2014).

Steve Van Remortel, *Stop Selling Vanilla Ice Cream: The Scoop on Increasing Profit by Differentiating Your Company Through Strategy and Talent* (Greenleaf Book Group Press, 2012).

Jack Welch with Suzy Welch, *Winning* (HarperCollins, 2005).

I also recommend Soundview Executive Book Summaries, a service that publishes book summaries in multiple formats to fit busy schedules: www.summary.com.

NOTES

1. "Grace Brewster Murray Hopper," Wikipedia, last modified September 15, 2015, https://en.wikipedia.org/wiki/Grace_Hopper

2. Philip Schieber, "The Wit and Wisdom of Grace Hopper," OCLC Newsletter, March/April 1987, No. 167, http://www.cs.yale.edu/homes/tap/Files/hopper-wit.html

3. Lewis Carroll, Alice's Adventures in Wonderland.

4. Benjamin Disraeli, The Infernal Marriage, part III (1834).

5. John C. Maxwell, "The Law of the Lid," The John Maxwell Co. Leadership Wired Blog, July 19, 2013, http://www.johnmaxwell.com/blog/the-law-of-the-lid

6. Tyson Foods, "Faith in the Workplace," http://www.tysonfoods.com/ways-we-care/faith-in-the-workplace.aspx

7. Hobby Lobby, "Our Story," http://www.hobbylobby.com/about-us/our-story

8. Mary Kay Ash, Mary Kay: You Can Have it All (Prima Lifestyles, 1995).

9. Abby Ohlheiser, "The World According to Chick-fil-A Founder Truett Cathy," Morning Mix, Washington Post, September 8, 2014, http://www.washingtonpost.com/news/morning-mix/wp/2014/09/08/the-world-according-to-chick-fil-a-founder-truett-cathy/

10. Zachary Crockett, "The Church of In-N-Out Burger," Priceonomics, September 8, 2014, http://priceonomics.com/the-church-of-in-n-out-burger/

11. Mark Borden and Anya Kamenetz, "Timberland's Jeff Swartz on Corporate Responsibility," Fast Company, September 2008, http://www.fastcompany.com/958580/timberlands-jeff-swartz-corporate-responsibility

12. Melissa Allison, "Alaska Airlines to Stop Handing Out Prayer Cards to Passengers," Seattle Times, originally published January 25, 2012, updated January 26, 2012, http://www.seattletimes.com/business/alaska-airlines-to-stop-handing-out-prayer-cards-to-passengers/

13. Edwin McDowell, "Bible Now Shares Hotel Rooms with Some Other Good Books," New York Times, December 26, 1995, http://www.nytimes.com/1995/12/26/us/bible-now-shares-hotel-rooms-with-some-other-good-books.html

14. Lisa LaMotta May, "Religious CEOs: JetBlue Founder, David Neeleman," Minyanville, May 19, 2010, http://www.minyanville.com/special-features/articles/religious-ceo-david-neeleman-jetblue-airlines/5/19/2010/id/28270

15. Interstate Batteries, "Our Purpose," accessed September 8, 2015, http://corporate.interstatebatteries.com/purpose_values/

16. William Pollard, "Honoring God at ServiceMaster," Christianity 9 to 5, from: The Soul of the Firm (Zondervan, 1996), http://www.christianity9to5.org/honoring-god-at-servicemaster/

17. Tom's of Maine, "Our Reason for Being," accessed September 2014, http://www.tomsofmaine.com/company/overlay/Our-Reason-For-Being

ABOUT THE AUTHOR

 W. Theodore "Theo" Etzel III is a Floridian, born in Miami. He graduated from Stetson University in DeLand, in 1980, with a bachelor of science in economics and finance from the university's School of Business and also ran the school's radio station.

After graduation, he worked for Days Inns of America in statewide real estate acquisition. He quickly advanced in the company and moved to Atlanta to serve as vice president of development.

While in Atlanta, Etzel also owned two Ben & Jerry's ice cream franchises and was on the staff of Habitat for Humanity, building homes and acquiring and rezoning land in north Fulton County for the organization.

In 1995, he moved to Naples, Florida, and assumed the position of president and CEO of Conditioned Air Corporation of Naples, Inc. At the time, it was a $2.7 million operation in the residential market. By 2015, the company had grown to a $45 million organization in the residential and light commercial market, with emergency service, contracts, production housing, retrofit, and custom design–build construction. Conditioned Air employs in excess of three hundred full-time workers and has branch offices in Fort Myers and Sarasota. In 2010, Conditioned Air received the National Contractor of the Year award from the Air Conditioning Contractors of America. In 2011, Conditioned Air was awarded the Uncommon Friends Foundation Business Ethics Award for its commitment to integrity in business practices.

Theo is part of Vistage, an international association of CEOs dedicated to constant improvement of business practices and personal development. He is a former chairman of the board for Grace Place for Children and Families in Naples, a faith-based charity that is committed to helping underprivileged and at-risk children attain higher learning and life skills through mentoring relationships. He is chairman of the board of Encore Bank, a community bank headquartered in Southwest Florida. In October 2011, Theo was inducted into the Junior Achievement Hall of Fame in Collier County, and the Collier County Champions for Learning named him a Man of Distinction in 2013.

He and his wife, Kim, have been married since 1980 and have two children—Chad and Kristen—who are each married and pursuing their own successful careers.